Canadian Oil Sands Investors' Guide

by

Derek S. Gates, CFA

Founder of the Sustainable Oil Sands Sector Index ™

Note for Librarians: A cataloguing record for this book is available from Library and Archives
Canada at www.collectionscanada.ca/amicus/index-e.html
ISBN 1-4251-0952-7

Printed in Victoria, BC, Canada. Printed on paper with minimum 30% recycled fibre.
Trafford's print shop runs on "green energy" from solar, wind and other environmentally-friendly power sources.

TRAFFORD
PUBLISHING™

Offices in Canada, USA, Ireland and UK

Book sales for North America and international:
Trafford Publishing, 6E–2333 Government St.,
Victoria, BC V8T 4P4 CANADA
phone 250 383 6864 (toll-free 1 888 232 4444)
fax 250 383 6804; email to orders@trafford.com
Book sales in Europe:
Trafford Publishing (UK) Limited, 9 Park End Street, 2nd Floor
Oxford, UK OX1 1HH UNITED KINGDOM
phone 44 (0)1865 722 113 (local rate 0845 230 9601)
facsimile 44 (0)1865 722 868; info.uk@trafford.com
Order online at:
trafford.com/06-2710

10 9 8 7 6 5 4 3 2 1

I dedicate this book to my wife, Darlene, who makes my life complete and to my son, Tyler, whom I place all my hopes for the future.

Table of Contents

Acknowledgements

This book has been a work in progress that is several years in the making. I would like to thank my wife, Darlene Gates, for her invaluable advice, support and encouragement during the writing of the book.

I would like to thank my long time associate, Brenda McNulty, for her work editing the manuscript and for her faith in the project.

My views on the oil sands have been shaped by many people over the years. I'd like to acknowledge the work that was done by John Mawdsley, a former research analyst at Raymond James Ltd. John was a strong advocate of the sector when it was unpopular with investors and is one of the most astute analysts I have ever met.

Dr. Pedro Pereira, Co Chair of the Alberta Ingenuity Centre for In Situ Energy provided great insight into the future of Canada's oil sands. The research conducted at the centre holds the promise of solving many of the issues with current oil sands extraction technology and a look forward to the many advances we can expect in the future.

Lastly, I would like to acknowledge the work by the Pembina Institute on the environmental issues related to the oil sands. I found their published reports and in depth analysis very informative.

Introduction

The global energy sector has been profoundly transformed in the last three years and a new trend is developing that promises to dominate the investment sector for decades to come. The new trend is the sustained and persistent rise in the price of the world's primary energy source, crude oil. Crude oil futures began trading on the NYMEX exchange in 1986 the price of West Texas Intermediate (WTI) crude oil has traded mostly between $10 and $40 with a long term average price of $20 per barrel[1]. Since 2003 the trend has changed dramatically due to three main factors that have combined to drive prices above the historical trend:

> **Declines in new oil discoveries**
> **Increases in global demand**
> **Lack of investment in oil industry infrastructure**

Oil discoveries peaked in the US in the 1930's and globally in the 1960's despite increased spending on exploration and advanced technologies for finding and extracting crude oil[2]. At the same time, global demand has been increasing steadily over the years and currently stands at 84.7 million barrels/day and is expected to grow to 98 million barrels/day by 2015[3]. The main driver for demand growth is the rapid industrialization of China and India and the continued rapid growth of North American demand. To make matters worse, the existing crude oil infrastructure is insufficient to handle the expected future demand. Investment in oil refineries, pipelines and supertanker ships is required to maintain and expand the supply of crude oil. In addition to these long term issues, we are faced with a world that is becoming increasingly dependent on the crude oil supplied by a handful of exporting countries. Of the 24 major oil exporting countries, the bulk of the production and reserves are located in politically unstable countries such as Venezuela, Nigeria, Sudan, Iraq, Iran, Russia and Saudi Arabia[4].

Despite these problems there is hope for the global economy and a major opportunity for investors. The global energy sector is shifting its focus to unconventional sources such as Natural Gas from Coal (NGC), shale oil and gas, arctic oil and gas and heavy oil deposits such as Canada's oil sands and Venezuela's heavy oil. Many of these unconventional resources are located in the consuming nations of North America and China and can be extracted economically at today's high energy prices. The focus of this book is to educate the reader on the most promising source of unconventional oil, Canada's oil sands deposit and to discuss in detail the tremendous investment opportunity it now represents.

In recent years Canada's Athabasca Oil Sands have attracted international attention from politicians, environmentalists, energy experts and investors. The intended audience for the _Canadian Oil Sands Investors' Guide_ is retail and institutional investors who are looking for a concise and informative guide to investing in the sector. This guide is designed to point investors in the right direction, highlight the main issues and to provide the reader with relevant information to evaluate the investment merits of the numerous oil sands related stocks.

This book is divided into four main parts that answer the key questions about Canada's Oil Sands resource:

Part I: What are Canada's Oil Sands?

Part II: Why Invest in Canada's Oil Sands?

Part III: What are the Opportunities and Risks?

Part IV: How Can You Invest in Canada's Oil Sands?

In the first part a brief history of the development of Canada's oil sands is discussed. In addition you will learn about the current extraction methods used by industry, discover the extent of the resource and how it compares to other oil reserves around the globe.

The second part makes the case for investing in Canada's oil sands sector. Current developments will be discussed and a detailed breakdown of the profitability of the sector will be estimated using current energy price levels. An overview of ongoing and planned expansions will be provided along with production forecasts for the next decade. Other issues discussed in this section include the economic and political stability of the province of Alberta (where most of the resource is based), the high leverage of oil sands producers to rising energy prices, the scale of the undeveloped reserves and recent technological advancements that will reduce cost and increase profitability.

The third part looks at the opportunities and risks that investors in this sector face. Topics range from capacity limits, labour and environment issues to geopolitical, technology and global oil supply and demand opportunities.

The final part of the book deals with directly investing in the sector. This part includes a description of the industry benchmark, Oil Sands Sector Index ™ and key company profiles. In addition, there are detailed discussions of different investment strategies such as growth and income investing, tracking the sector, outperforming the S&P/TSX Capped Energy index benchmark, and reducing your investment risks through a hedging.

It is my sincere hope that you enjoy reading this book as much as I enjoyed writing it.

Sincerely,

Derek S. Gates, CFA
Founder of the Sustainable Oil Sands Sector Index ™

Part I: What are Canada's Oil Sands?

A Brief History of Oil Sands Development in Canada

There have been four epochs of development of Canada's oil sands which I separate into four distinct phases:

Exploration Phase	1700	to	1919
Scientific Phase	1920	to	1929
Testing Phase	1930	to	1959
Commercialization Phase	1960	to	1997

Since 1997, the rapid expansion of the oil sands operations in Northern Alberta is creating a fifth phase of development that is best characterized as mass industrialization which will be discussed in more detail in Part II of the book. The following is a brief historical timeline of the key events that marked the phase of development.[5]

Exploration Phase 1700 to 1919

1719 - A member of the Cree First Nations brings the first sample of oil sands to the Hudson Bay post at Fort Churchill.

1778 – An explorer named Peter Pond discovers the oil sands seeping through rock outcroppings along the river banks in Northern Alberta and observes that the Aboriginal people use the material to waterproof their canoes.

1875 - John Macoun, a botanist for the Geological Survey of Canada observes the rivers draining into Lake Athabasca are naturally washing oil out of the oil sands. He observed that the tar wasn't mixed with mineral matter, instead that the tar flowed through it. This is the basis for today's technology for extracting bitumen from oil sands.

1883 - First attempt to separate bitumen from oil sand with the use of water was attempted by G.C. Hoffman of the Geological Survey of Canada.

1906 – Count Alfred von Hammerstein drills for oil in the Fort McMurray area but finds salt deposits instead. Between 1906 and 1913, salt was the only commercial product to come from the area.

1913 - Sydney Ells uses bitumen as a road surfacing material. He convinces a joint federal-provincial-municipal venture to pave roads in Edmonton, Alberta. Also, with the help of the Mellon Institute of Industrial Research, extraction processes for separating the oil from oil sands were developed using heated water and reagents.

Scientific Phase 1920 to 1929

1920 – Dr. Karl Clark joined the Research Council of Alberta and began working on oil sand separation methods.

1921 – The Scientific and Industrial Research Council of Alberta was formed to research mineral deposits, coal resources and the tar sands. It was the first government research council in Canada.

1921 – The Alcan Oil Company drills for oil in the Bitumount area about 90 kilometers north of Fort McMurray.

1922 – Dr. Karl Clark and his associate Sidney Blair build a small separation unit in the basement of the University of Alberta power plant.

1925 – Thomas Draper begins experimenting with oil sands as a paving material, untreated or mixed with asphalt. The paving material was used on part of Parliament Hill in Ottawa.

1925 – Robert Fitzsimmons constructs model hot-water separation plant at Bitumount site.

1927 – Alcan Oil Company becomes the International Bitumen Company under Robert Fitzsimmons control. After unsuccessful drilling results, he concludes that surface extraction would be the best commercial process.

1928 – Dr. Clark and Sidney Blair are granted a Canadian patent for the hot water oil sand separation process they invented.

1929 – Robert Fitzsimmons produces a roofing tar used in Edmonton, Alberta from his Bitumount site. He later produced the first refined commercial fuels from the oil sands but used up all of his capital reserves in development expenses and had to shut down the site between 1932 and 1937.

Testing Phase 1930 to 1959

1930 – The Canadian Northern Oil Company, controlled by Max Ball, Basil Jones and James McClave, applied for several oil sands leases in the Horse River and Athabasca region. Later, the company was renamed Abasand Oils Ltd.

1930 – Robert Fitzsimmons makes the first sale of commercially produced bitumen in Edmonton, Alberta.

1936 – The Bitumount plant is improved and expanded and a new refinery is constructed. Also, the Abasand Oils plant was completed with an operating capacity of 250 tons per day. The Abasand process combined a solvent extraction with hot water extraction in a two stage process.

1941 – The Abasand plant began operating on a regular basis after several years of delays and technical problems. Unfortunately, the plant was burned down in November of that year and took three years to be rebuilt.

1942 - Lloyd Champion purchased International Bitumen from Fitzsimmons and renamed it Oil Sands Ltd. By 1948 the Bitumount plant had recommenced operations.

1944 – After three long years, the Abasand plant was reconstructed along with the refinery later in the year.

1945 – After less than a year of operation, a welder's torch accidentally ignited some oil near the separation plant at Abasand Oils Ltd. Again, the plant was destroyed including all the support structures.

1949 – The province of Alberta takes over the Bitumount site.

1951 – Alberta hosts its first Athabasca Oil Sands Conference.

1953 – Oil Sands Ltd. is restructured into a consortium including Abasand Oils, Canadian Oils Ltd., Champion's Oil Sands Ltd., and Sun Oil Co. of Philadelphia.

1954 – Alberta sells the Bitumount plant to CanAmera Oil Sands which used it for testing.

1957 - CanAmera sells the Bitumount plant to Royalite Oil Company.

1958 – Royalite closes down operations at Bitumount site.

Commercialization Phase 1960 to 1997

1962 – The Great Canadian Oil Sands Company begins construction of the first large-scale commercial plant at a site north of Fort McMurray called Mildred-Ruth Lake. The main plant was built between 1964 and 1967 and could produce over 31,000 barrels per day.

1964 – Syncrude Canada Ltd. is incorporated.

1967 – Great Canadian Oil Sands Company officially opens on September 30 with the Premier of Alberta, Ernest Manning presiding over the ceremonies.

1974 – Syncrude becomes a joint public-private venture, sponsored by Esso Resources (Imperial Oil), Gulf Canada, Canada Cities Service, Hudson's Bay Oil and Gas, and the Alberta and Canadian governments. Construction of the plant took over 4 years and had a design capacity of over 125,000 barrels of oil per day.

1974 – The Alberta Oil Sands Technology and Research Authority (AOSTRA) was established.

1978 – On September 15, Syncrude's new oil sands plant officially opened at Mildred Lake.

1979 – The Great Canadian Oil Sands plant was renamed Suncor Inc., Oil Sands Group.

1983 – AOSTRA developed its own detailed designs for an Underground Test Facility project for testing in-situ (deep underground) extraction techniques. The mandate of the organization was to develop methods to recover the vast majority of the oil sands that are too deep for surface mining. The organization pioneered the Steam-Assisted Gravity Drainage (SAGD) process that is in use today.

1993 – Suncor replaces bucketwheel excavators with truck and shovel equipment for oil sands mining.

1995 – Suncor and Syncrude announce plans for expansion. Syncrude's new "Aurora" mine site is located about 35 kilometers northeast of the Mildred Lake site and begins operations in 2001. Suncor's "Steepbank Mine" will be located on the east side of the Athabasca River.

1997 – On March 10, Suncor Inc., Oil Sands Group is renamed Suncor Energy.

1997 – On March 14, Shell Canada announces plans to develop a new $1 billion oil sands operation on Lease 13, located about 70 kilometers north of Fort McMurray. On April 25, Mobil Oil Canada announces plans to develop another $1 billion oil sands project on Lease 36 located north of Fort McMurray.

1997 – On September 24, the Alberta government enacts the Generic Oil Sands Royalty Regime. This act eliminates all other government subsidies for oil sands development, creates an open and fair market for all private companies to develop the oil sands and clears the way for over $60 billion dollars in oil sands projects into 2010. This new royalty regime reduced the royalty rate to oil sands producers to 1% until all capital costs of their projects are recovered. This marks the beginning of the modern era of development of Canada's oil sands.

2000 – The Alberta Energy Research Institute (AERI) is established and takes over the research programs previously administered by AOSTRA.

2001 – The Athabasca Oil Sands Project, a consortium involving Shell Canada, Chevron Canada, and Western Oil Sands begins operating north of Mildred Lake.

2003- The Alberta government releases a report on water resources named, *Water for Life: Alberta's Strategy for Sustainability*

2005 Deer Creek Energy is purchased by Total SA of France

2006 Blackrock Ventures is purchased by Shell Canada

How big is the resource in Canada?

Canada's Oil Sands represent one of the largest reserves of crude oil in the world. Based on current recovery technologies, development and economics there is an estimated 174 billion barrels of recoverable oil in Canada's three main oil sands regions (see Figure #1).[6]

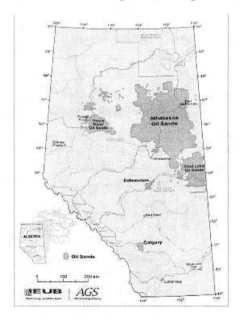

Figure #1: Alberta's Key Oil Sands Regions, Source: Alberta Geological Survey, Energy Utilities Board

The Athabasca Oil Sands region holds the largest resource and is the closest to the surface which allows for surface mining extraction. How does this resource compare with other known oil reserves in the world? Canada's Oil Sands reserves are number two in the world behind only Saudi Arabia which claims reserves of 260 billion barrels of oil (see Figure #2).

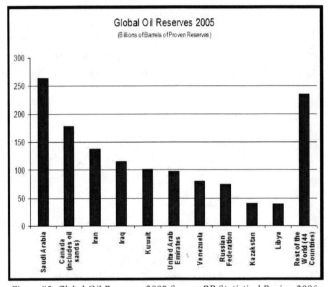

Figure #2: Global Oil Reserves, 2005 Source: BP Statistical Review 2006

The estimated 174 billion barrels of recoverable oil from Canada's oil sands is expected to increase in the future as new leases are developed, more advanced extraction technologies are implemented and as higher oil prices improve the profit margins of oil sands producers. The total resource base in the region is between 1.7 to 2.5 trillion barrels of oil according to the Alberta government estimates of which only 10% is currently considered recoverable and less than 3% has been produced to date.[7]

How is the oil extracted?

Canada's Oil Sands are an extremely heavy oil, or bitumen (see Figure #3). The key characteristic of the oil sands is the high viscosity (resistance to flow) and high density. The US Department of Energy considers heavy oil to have a density range of 10 to 22 degrees of specific gravity according to American Petroleum Industry (API) standards.[8] The light sweet crude oil that is found in Texas (West Texas Intermediary) and Saudi Arabia is considered the highest quality due to the ease of refining the oil into other products such as gasoline and heating oil. Light oil has a density range of 35 to 40+ API. Canada's oil sands (originally named tar sands) are significantly denser with a range between 6 and 10 degrees API. In addition to the high density, producers of Canada's oil sands have difficulty getting the oil to flow because of the high viscosity. The oil sands have at least 100 times the viscosity of conventional oil which makes transportation by pipeline difficult without diluents (gas-liquids that are mixed with the bitumen to reduce the viscosity and allow pipeline transportation).

Figure #3: Bitumen in raw form,
Photo: Sustainable Wealth Management Ltd.

The two known extraction methodologies for Canada's oil sands are mining and in-situ. Mining is the preferred method when the resource is close to the surface. The generally accepted maximum depth of the mining approach is about 250 feet deep. About 20% of Canada's 174 billion barrels of recoverable oil sands can be accessed using the mining approach.[9] In-Situ (Latin for "in place") methods are used when the oil sands deposit are buried deep in the ground. In situ technology is relatively new approach to extracting oil sands and is expected to catch up to mining production in the next 15 to 20 years.

Mining Method

The mining method is the most prevalent method of extracting Canada's Oil Sands. This method is most applicable to oil sands deposits that are within 250 feet of the surface (see Figure #4). The Athabasca region has oil sands resources that are close enough to the surface to apply mining techniques.

Figure #4: Oil Sands Bucket Shovel,
Photo: Sustainable Wealth Management Ltd.

Mining for oil sands leaves a huge footprint on the landscape. Excavation and removal of the overburden (trees, vegetation, wetlands) is necessary to get to the oil deposit. Approximately four tones of material (50% soil & rock, 50% oil sands) must be unearthed to produce one barrel (42 Gallons) of synthetic crude oil. The hydraulic shovels depicted in Figure #4 can move over 1400 cu ft of material per scoop and it takes three loads to fill up the massive Caterpillar 797 trucks.[10] The trucks weigh more than a Boeing 747, are 50 ft long and 23 ft tall and have tires that are twice the height of Michael Jordan (13 feet tall). Figure #5 compares the mining trucks to regular sized trucks. The mining process can recover up to 90% of the bitumen found in the deposit and the remainder is unrecoverable and diverted to settling pools called tailings ponds. The mining process requires waste quantities of water (2 to 5 barrels of fresh water) and natural gas (250 cu ft +) for each barrel of synthetic crude produced and the land must be reclaimed after mining operations are completed. Commercial size mining operations have been in existence since 1967 with the opening of the Sun Oil mine (now called Suncor Energy).

Figure #5: Oil Sands Mining Trucks, Photo:
Sustainable Wealth Management Ltd.

In Situ Method

There are two in situ methods currently in use; the Steam Assisted Gravity Drainage (SAGD) and Cyclic Steam Stimulation (CSS) method. Both methods are designed to extract bitumen deposits that are trapped too deep in the ground for traditional mining methods. Figure #6 demonstrates the SAGD method of oil sands extraction.

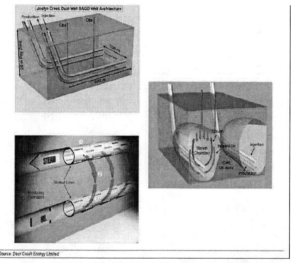

Figure #6: Diagram of SAGD In Situ Extraction Method,
Source: Deer Creek Energy Ltd.

In situ methods are the key to unlocking the vast potential of Canada's oil sands. The majority of the oil sands deposits are too deep for surface mining extraction methods. The growth of oil sands projects will be driven by in situ production methods. According to the Alberta government, 93% of oil sands reserves are designated as in-situ.[11]

Figure #7 details the current split of extraction methods employed in Canada's oil sands. Current breakdown by extraction methodology is 70% mining and 30% in situ but this is expected to even out to a 50 – 50 split by 2020 as the growth of in situ production outpaces the expansion of mining projects.

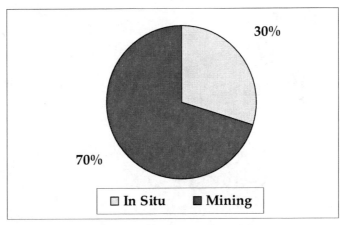

Figure #7: Extraction Methods – Canada's Oil Sands by Production, Source Sustainable Wealth Management Ltd., company reports

Part II: Why Invest in Canada's Oil Sands?

Current Developments

Since the new oil sands royalty regime was introduced by the Alberta government in 1997 there has been over $87 billion dollars invested or committed to oil sands projects up to 2016.[12] Table #1 summarizes Canada's oil sands production by extraction method and Table #2 summarizes potential oil sands production if all announced projects are completed by 2020.

Table #1: Existing Canadian Oil Sands Project Summary

Extraction Method	Current Production	Number of Projects	Avg. Production per Project
Mining	751,000 boe/day	3	250,000 boe/day
In Situ	324,000 boe/day	8	40,500 boe/day
Total	**1,075,000 boe/day**	**11**	**97,700 boe/day**

Table #2: Future Canadian Oil Sands Project Summary (by 2020)

Extraction Method	Current Production	Number of Projects	Avg. Production per Project
Mining	2,695,000 boe/day	8	337,000 boe/day
In Situ	2,772,000 boe/day	29	96,000 boe/day
Total	**5,467,000 boe/day**	**37**	**147,750 boe/day**

In Table #2 we see that Canada's oil sands could potentially reach 5.5 million barrels of oil per day by 2020. It should be noted that this figure is dependent on 17 projects representing over 1.8 million barrels of oil production progressing beyond the planning and development stage.

This section will only focus on the 9 projects (1 Mining, 8 In Situ) that are approved and under construction as of mid 2006.

Table #3: List of Canadian Oil Sands Projects Under Construction

Project Name	Owner(s)	Extraction Method	Initial Production	Future Production	Expected Start up
Surmont	Conoco Philips/Total	In Situ	27,000 boe/day	200,000 boe/day	2006
Tucker Lake	Husky Energy	In Situ	35,000 boe/day	35,000 boe/day	2006
Joslyn Creek	Total/Enerplus	In Situ	10,000 boe/day	40,000 boe/day	2006
Long Lake	OPTI/Nexen	In Situ	58,500 boe/day	117,000 boe/day	2007
Christina Lake	MEG Energy (Private Co.)	In Situ	3,000 boe/day	140,000 boe/day	2007
Orion	Shell Canada	In Situ	10,000 boe/day	20,000 boe/day	2007
Great Divide	Connacher	In Situ	10,000 boe/day	30,000 boe/day	2007
Jackfish	Devon Energy	In Situ	35,000 boe/day	70,000 boe/day	2007
Horizon	Canadian Natural Resources	Mining	110,000 boe/day	435,000 boe/day	2008
			298,500 boe/day	**1,087,000 boe/day**	

As you can see from Table #3 these 9 projects will more than double Canada's oil sands production once they hit their target production rates. One of the projects merits further attention. Long Lake project, owned by OPTI Canada and Nexen is unique in that it is the first commercial application of the OrCrude™ Technology. This technology promises to reduce/eliminate the amount of natural gas used by in situ oil sands producers through a process that can gasify asphaltene (residual product of refining bitumen). In addition, the facility will produce hydrogen for the refining process, generate its own electricity and fully upgrade the bitumen to a high quality synthetic crude oil (SCO).

The advantage of this set up is that the project will not be exposed to rising input costs from high natural gas prices, bitumen discounts and the need for diluent for pipeline transportation. The project managers feel that their operating costs will be in the $5 to $9 US cost per barrel[13] which would make this project one of the lowest cost operators in the sector. This project will form the template for the next generation of in situ oil sands projects.

Profitability

The profitability of oil sands producers is constantly changing and differs from project to project. In this section we will discuss the profitability of several types of oil sands projects using the four most important factors; current crude oil prices, natural gas prices, quality differential (price discount of heavy oil vs. light, sweet crude), and project cost overruns. Other factors that are important but ignored for this calculation were US to Canadian dollar exchange rates, diluent usage & cost, project delays, time to reach full production, interest rates, labour costs and environmental costs (Kyoto protocols). For simplicity, these costs will be lumped into one figure for each project and assumed to remain relatively stable compared to swings in crude oil and natural gas prices.

The analysis will give you a snapshot of the profitability of the following four types of oil sands projects:

1) Mining project with full upgrader (synthetic crude oil production)
2) In situ project with full upgrader (synthetic crude oil production)
3) In situ project without upgrader (bitumen production only)
4) In situ project with full upgrading and gasification (synthetic crude oil production)

You will notice that there is no analysis of a mining project without an upgrader. The reasoning is that most of these projects involve multi-billion dollar investments and the long term benefits of capturing the bitumen to crude oil differential outweigh the additional capital cost incurred.

The following sections will discuss the importance of crude oil prices, natural gas prices, crude oil quality differentials and project cost overruns on the profitability of oil sands operations.

Crude Oil Prices

By far the most important factor in the profitability equation is the price of conventional crude oil. Low prices have historically indicated excess supply, low demand or both and made it extremely difficult for oil sands producers to breakeven. However, the current high price environment is excellent for the development of Canada's oil sands and their current profitability. The uptrend is a result of growing global demand[14], depletion of existing reserves[15] and a lack of growth in new oil supplies[16]. As you can see in Figure #8, most spikes in oil prices were short lived in the 1980s & 1990s but the recent upturn since 2002 has been sustained. In the author's opinion, this trend will remain in force for another decade or more until the global supply comfortably exceeds global demand for crude oil.

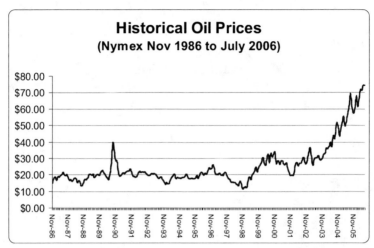

Figure #8: Historical Crude Oil Prices, 1986 - 2006, Source: Bloomberg,
Sustainable Wealth Management

Natural Gas Prices

Natural gas use is a major cost for oil sands producers. Natural gas is used to heat up the water that is used to separate the bitumen from the oil sands in mining projects. It is also used in the upgrading process to convert the bitumen to synthetic crude oil. For in situ projects, natural gas is used to create steam that is directly injected in the reservoir to lower the viscosity of the bitumen. In all oil sands projects, you will find that the cost of natural gas is one of the largest variable costs.

As you can see in Figure #9, natural gas prices are on the rise in North America. Fortunately for oil sands producers, price spikes have been short lived, however, the long term trend is rising. Companies that can use natural gas more efficiently or can eliminate the use of natural gas in the production of Canada's oil sands will have a significant cost advantage in the future. Natural gas is the largest operating expense for in situ oil sands projects, representing 60% of all operating costs[17]. Mining operations use far less natural gas but it still represents 15% of total operating costs.

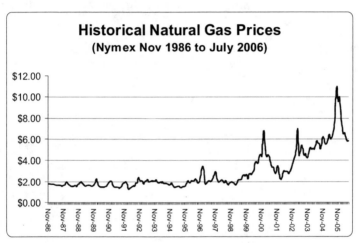

Figure #9: Historical Natural Gas Prices, 1986 - 2006, Source: Bloomberg, Sustainable Wealth Management Ltd.

Quality Differential

Oil sands producers produce two types of products, bitumen and synthetic crude oil. Synthetic crude oil is high quality oil that can be easily refined into other products such as gasoline, heating oil and jet fuel. Synthetic crude oil trades near or sometimes above the price level of light, sweet crude. Bitumen is a tar like substance that requires expensive upgrading and refining before it can be converted into more useful products. This additional upgrading and refining cost is adjusted by discounting the price of bitumen to the price of oil. In Figure #10 shows that bitumen has traded between 50%

and 90% of the value of light sweet crude over the last 10 years[18].   As conventional supplies of light sweet crude decline, refineries will be redesigned to handle heavier oil from Canada's oil sands. Demand for bitumen to replace conventional crude oil supplies will narrow the bitumen to crude oil differential to the 70% to 80% range long term. Currently, the historical average over the last 10 years has been 68%.

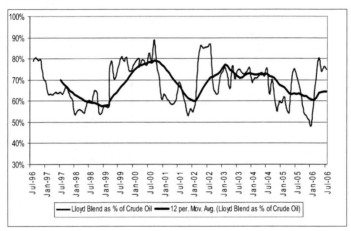

Figure #10: Heavy Oil as a % of Crude Oil Prices, 1996 - 2006, Source: Bloomberg, Sustainable Wealth Management Ltd.

Project Cost Overruns

Cost overruns are a major problem for Canadian oil sands producers. The reasons for cost overruns range from materials and skilled labour shortages to building in a remote and cold environment. The biggest cause of cost overruns is the pressure of having to build several mega-projects in a short period of time in a remote location with limited infrastructure.   Cost overruns are corrosive to investor returns as they dramatically increase the initial capital cost of a project, reduce rates of return on invested capital and lengthen the payback period of a project. Table #4 highlights the cost overruns in recent oil sands projects:

Table #4: Recent Oil Sands Projects: Cost Overruns

Owners	Project	Initial Cost	Revised Cost	% Cost Overrun	Additional Production	Cost per barrel
Shell, Western Oil Sands, Chevron	Athabasca Oil Sands Project	$7.3 Billion	$11 Billion	51%	100,000 b/day Synthetic Crude Oil	$110,000 per barrel
Canadian Natural Resources	Horizon Oil Sands Project	$8.5 Billion	$10.5 Billion	24%	110,000 b/day Synthetic Crude Oil	$95,500 per barrel
Various, Joint Venture	Syncrude Expansion	$5.7 Billion	$8.3 Billion	46%	112,000 b/day Synthetic Crude Oil	$74,100 per barrel
Nexen/OPTI	Long Lake	$3.4 Billion	$3.4 Billion	0%	60,000 b/day Synthetic Crude Oil	$56,700 per barrel

Table #4 summarizes cost overruns on current oil sands projects. The Nexen/OPTI Long Lake project is on budget but is still two years away from completion. All the other projects have experienced delays and cost overruns that have impacted rates of return on capital for investors. However, some of the projects such as the AOSP, Horizon and Syncrude Expansion are laying the groundwork for future expansion which might account for the higher up front costs. Another important factor to consider is that the three larger projects are mining related while the Long Lake project is an in situ (SAGD method) project. Other in situ oil sands projects such as Imperial Oil Cold Lake and Husky Energy's Tucker Lake project have come in on time and on budget.

Profitability Analysis of Canada's Oil Sands Producers

Most oil and gas analysts that cover the Canadian oil sands producers develop their own models to determine the profitability of each company. Generally, the projections show that at crude oil prices above $30 to $40 US per barrel that the majority of the oil sands producers have rates of return on invested capital in excess of 15% per annum[19]. Many of the profitability models published by brokerages have not caught up to current crude oil pricing levels because analysts are reluctant to predict today's high oil prices into the future. This profitability model is based on the current market environment. It uses historical averages and commodity futures prices out to 2011 to determine the profitability of the typical oil sands operation. Any oil sands producer can arrange to lock in these prices today and essentially reduce their commodity price risk while securing today's high rates of return. Table #5 outlines the assumptions used in the profitability model.

Table #5: Key Assumptions: Oil Sands Profitability

Project Type	Project Size and Cost	Crude Oil Prices	Natural Gas Prices	Bitumen Prices	% Cost Overrun	Natural Gas Usage	Non Energy Operating Costs
Mining Project with Upgrader	100,000 boe/day SCO $5.5 Billion	Futures Prices as of Aug 18, 2006	Futures Prices as of Aug 18, 2006	No Discount for SCO	50%	0.70 mm btu per barrel	21 % of Crude Oil Prices
In Situ Project with Upgrader & Gasification	60,000 boe/day SCO $3.4 Billion	Futures Prices as of Aug18, 2006	Futures Prices as of Aug18, 2006	No Discount for SCO	30%	0.02 mm btu per barrel	12 % of Crude Oil Prices
In Situ Project with Upgrader	60,000 boe/day SCO $2.8 Billion	Futures Prices as of Aug18, 2006	Futures Prices as of Aug18, 2006	No Discount for SCO	20%	1.20 mm btu per barrel	10 % of Crude Oil Prices
In Situ Project without Upgrader	60,000 boe/day Bitumen $1.5 Billion	Futures Prices as of Aug18, 2006	Futures Prices as of Aug18, 2006	10 Year History 68% of Crude	15%	1.00 mm btu per barrel	7 % of Crude Oil Prices

Another key assumption is that each project is 100% equity financed. In reality, most projects are 50% financed which gives investors a higher return on invested capital.

Figure #11 is based on new projects coming within the original budget estimates. The drop off in rates of return after the 2 or 3 year mark reflects the increase in Alberta Royalty Tax Regime after the projects have recovered all capital costs. The rates of return on capital invested in today's market environment are exceptional.

The biggest surprise was the profitability of bitumen producers. Bitumen producers are at the mercy of high natural gas prices, high bitumen to crude oil price differentials and volatile swings in crude oil prices. You should note that at the time of this analysis the market environment was more favorable to bitumen producers mainly because crude oil is trading at 12 times natural gas prices, substantially above the historical trading ratio of 7 to 1. In addition, bitumen differentials have narrowed recently and demand for all sources of oil has climbed.

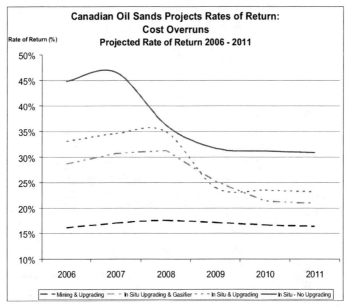

Figure #11: Rate of Return on Invested Capital, Projections from 2006 to 2011, No Cost Overruns, Source: Bloomberg, NYMEX, Sustainable Wealth Management Ltd., Various Company reports.

In reality most projects are exceeding their budget by a substantial margin. Figure #12 details the same projections after taking into account recent cost overruns.

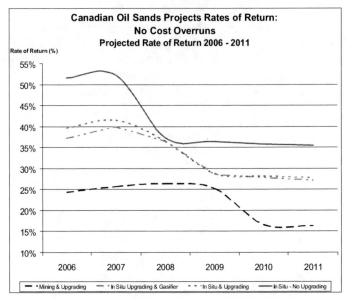

Figure #12: Rate of Return on Invested Capital, Projections from 2006 to 2011, After Cost Overruns, Source: Bloomberg, NYMEX, Sustainable Wealth Management Ltd., Various Company reports

Cost overruns have a detrimental effect on investment returns. Table #6 shows the impact of cost overruns in terms of lower rates of return and longer payback periods.

Table #6: Oil Sands Profitability Model Comparison

Project Type	Payback Period (On Budget)	Payback Period (Cost Overruns)	Delay in Achieving Payback	Reduction in Return on Capital
Mining Project with Upgrader	1439 Days or 3.9 Years	2166 Days or 5.9 Years	727 Days or 2.0 Years	5.6%
In Situ Project with Upgrader & Gasification	960 Days or 2.6 Years	1233 Days or 3.4 Years	273 Days or 0.75 Years	6.5%
In Situ Project with Upgrader	920 Days or 2.5 Years	1069 Days or 2.9 Years	149 Days or 0.4 years	4.9%
In Situ Project without Upgrader	704 Days or 1.9 Years	817 Days or 2.2 Years	113 Days or 0.3 Years	4.6%

According to my research, smaller projects are less likely to experience significant cost overruns. Building complex facilities such as a bitumen upgrader can add costs and delays to an oil sands project. In all cases, delays in reaching full production and escalating costs are detrimental to the rate of return on invested capital.

Expansion Plans

Table #3 described oil sands projects that are near completion. Those projects will double Canada's oil sands production from the current 1,000,000 + boe/day to in excess of 2,000,000 boe/day by the end of 2008. This section will discuss projects that are expected to be completed between 2009 and 2015. This analysis is highly subjective because of the volatility of the many factors involved. The projections described in Table #7 & 8 are dependent on crude prices remaining high, demand for crude remaining high, government tax incentives remaining as is, no further environmental restrictions and many other factors.

Table #7: Mining Expansion Plans 2009 to 2015

Project Name	Owner(s)	Extraction Method	Initial Production	Future Production	Expected Start up
Kearl Lake	Imperial Oil/ ExxonMobil	Mining	100,000 boe/day	300,000 boe/day	2010
Fort Hills	Petro-Canada /UTS/Teck-Cominco	Mining	100,000 boe/day	200,000 boe/day	2011
Joslyn Creek	Total/ Enerplus	Mining	50,000 boe/day	200,000 boe/day	2011
Northern Lights	Synenco/ Sinopec	Mining	50,000 boe/day	100,000 boe/day	2011
			75,000 boe/day	**200,000 boe/day**	

The mining projects are significantly larger operations than the planned in situ projects. The recent concern over higher construction costs at the Athabasca Oil Sands Project (Shell/Chevron/Western Oil Sands) has greatly impacted the prospects for these future mining projects. On average, initial production costs of $75,000+ per flowing barrel of synthetic crude oil (SCO) are now projected to increase by 33%, exceeding $100,000 per flowing barrel of SCO. Based on these cost figures the projects above might require up to $80 billion in capital expenditures between 2010 and 2020 for the additional 800,000 barrels of SCO production. All of these projects are in the planning and engineering stage of development and they are vulnerable to adverse events such as further cost increases, lower crude oil prices and environmental/governmental restrictions which might change/alter the decision to proceed.

Table #8: In Situ Expansion Plans 2009 to 2015

Project Name	Owner(s)	Extraction Method	Initial Production	Future Production	Expected Start up
Sunrise	Husky Energy	In Situ	50,000 boe/day	200,000 boe/day	2009
Kai Kos Dehseh	N.A. Oil Sands (Private)	In Situ	10,000 boe/day	160,000 boe/day	2009
Halfway Creek	Value Creation (Private)	In Situ	10,000 boe/day	40,000 boe/day	2009
Meadow Creek	Petro-Canada/ Nexen	In Situ	34,000 boe/day	34,000 boe/day	2009
Lewis	Petro-Canada	In Situ	34,000 boe/day	34,000 boe/day	2009
Borealis	Encana	In Situ	Not Announced	100,000 boe/day	2010
Kirby	Cdn Natural Resources	In Situ	30,000 boe/day	30,000 boe/day	2011
Birch Mountain	Cdn Natural Resources	In Situ	25,000 boe/day	75,000 boe/day	2013
Leismer	OPTI/ Nexen	In Situ	Not Announced	61,500 boe/day	2013
Cotton-wood	OPTI/ Nexen	In Situ	Not Announced	61,500 boe/day	2013
Gregoire	Cdn Natural Resources	In Situ	30,000 boe/day	102,000 boe/day	2015 – 2016
Whitesand /Orion	Petrobank	In Situ	10,000 boe/day	50,000 boe/day	2015+
			233,000 boe/day	**948,000 boe/day**	

On average, in situ projects are significantly smaller than their mining counterparts but in total they will add more to Canada's oil sands production between 2009 and 2015. They are also easier to start small and scale up, have lower startup costs and leave less of a visible environmental footprint. Technological advancements that reduce their operating costs and improve recovery rates are expected in the next 10 to 20 years. Also, the majority of Canada's oil sands reserves can only be extracted through the in situ methods.

Increasing Production

Conventional oil production is declining in many oil producing nations and is flat globally. It has been estimated by ExxonMobil that mature conventional oil producing wells currently experience a 6% to 8% decline in production every year[20]. To offset this decline in production and to keep up with growing global demand, oil producers must find and develop more oil each and every year. Figure #13 illustrates the impact of a 4% per annum production decline in a world that requires 2% more oil each and every year.

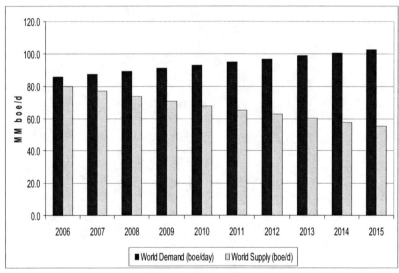

Figure #13: Projection of World Oil Supply vs. Demand, 2006 - 2015, Source: IEA, Sustainable Wealth Management Ltd.

Our challenge over the next decade is to economically develop new oil resources to meet this potential supply shortfall. Canada's oil sands will be a major new source of crude oil supplies just when the world is most desperately in need of additional oil. Figure #14 highlights the potential growth in Canada's oil sands production over the next 10 years.

The projections in Figure #14 are based on optimistic assumptions that project delays, cost overruns, labour shortages and volatile energy prices will not derail any of the planned projects. Conservative projections indicate that 2015 production will be closer to 3,300,000 barrels of oil equivalent per day. This still represents a tripling of production over a 10 year period, a compound growth rate of approximately 12% per year. This will help offset the decline in global conventional oil production mentioned earlier in this chapter.

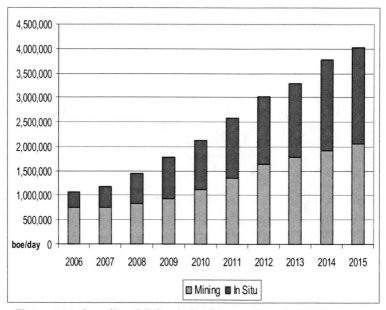

Figure #14: Canadian Oil Sands Production Growth, 2006 - 2015, Source: Company reports, Sustainable Wealth Management Ltd. estimates

Another consideration is the annual growth rate of oil sands production. Figure #15 clearly shows that the strongest growth phase is between 2006 and 2009. In addition, the fastest growing extraction method in the next decade for Canada's oil sands is the in situ methodology. In situ production is expected to grow by

20% per year while mining production is only expected to grow by 11% per year[21].

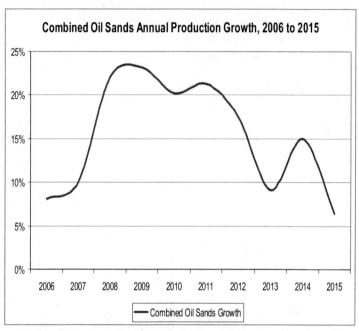

Figure #15: Canadian Oil Sands Annual Production Growth Rates, 2006 - 2015, Source: Company reports, Sustainable Wealth Management Ltd. estimates

Significant Undeveloped Reserves

The Alberta Energy Utilities Board estimates that Canada's oil sands represent 174 billion barrels of proven reserves and potentially 305 billion barrels of proven and probable reserves[22]. To date, approximately 5 Billion barrels of the original 179 Billion barrel initial established reserve has been produced, which means that 97% of the resource is still waiting to be exploited. Table #9 illustrates the vastness of the oil sands reserves.

Table #9: Oil Sands Reserves, Current Production Rates

	Reserves	Production Rate (boe/d)	Years of Production at Peak Rate
Current Reserves under development	83.9 Billion boe	1,060,000 boe/day	217
Total Proven Reserves	174 Billion boe	1,060,000 boe/day	452
Total Proven & Probable Reserves	305 Billion boe	1,060,000 boe/day	788

The problem with Canada's oil sands is that the development rate is too slow. Increasing production to 4 million boe/day rate will allow for at least 60 years of peak production. The current projects have discovered enough oil sands reserves to keep them producing at peak levels for over 55 years and they have the potential to develop another 91 billion barrels on their existing unexplored leases.

As illustrated in Figure #2, Canada's oil sands reserves are truly a world class resource that is just now being recognized. The key for oil sands producers is to maximize the production as soon as possible to capitalize on the growing global demand for oil.

High Leverage to Oil Prices

One of the greatest benefits of Canada's oil sands is the high leverage producers have to the rise in crude oil prices. Oil sands producers have enjoyed outstanding profit margins ever since oil prices exceeded the $35 to $40 per barrel price level on a consistent basis in 2004.

Existing oil sands producers have large, up front start up costs but are not exposed to increasing finding and development costs and their production profile does not decline like conventional oil wells. This translates into incredible free cash flow once initial costs have been recovered. Current oil sands projects have operating costs in the $10 to $20 US range per barrel of oil production. Recent high oil prices have accelerated the payback period for the initial cost outlays and many existing projects have already recovered all their capital costs.

This is translating into higher stock prices and gives oil sands producers the ability to self finance their next expansion phase.

In Figure #16 I compare the rise in crude oil prices over the last two years to the rise in ExxonMobil's stock price. Exxon provided investors with only a 53% gain while crude oil prices more than doubled. The main culprit for Exxon's underperformance is the poor leverage it has to the rise in oil prices. Last year, ExxonMobil spent $17 Billion US to maintain production at the 4.1 million boe/day rate and allocated another $23 Billion US in stock repurchases and dividend payments. In my opinion, the lack of investment opportunities is making it difficult to grow Exxon's oil production and has been holding back its stock appreciation.

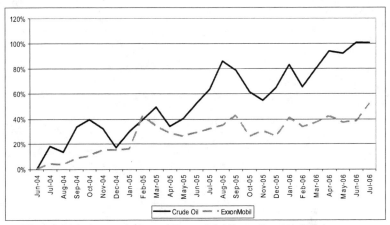

*Figure #16: Appreciation of ExxonMobil vs. Crude oil Prices,
June 2004 – Jul 2006, Source: Bloomberg*

Figure #17 clearly demonstrates that oil sands producers have excellent leverage to the rise in crude oil prices. After 6 months of crude oil prices trading above the $40 US level in the second half of 2004, Canadian oil sands producers started to consistently outperform crude oil. The main reason for this is the tremendous profit that oil sands producers generate once they recover their initial capital investment and oil prices remain above their variable operating costs. In addition, the market has recognized that their production will not decline for decades to come and that they have room to grow production and increase their recoverable oil reserves in the future. Over the last two years, the index of oil sands producers has gained a stunning 186% which is 85% better than the gain in crude oil prices and 133% higher than the gain in ExxonMobil's shares.

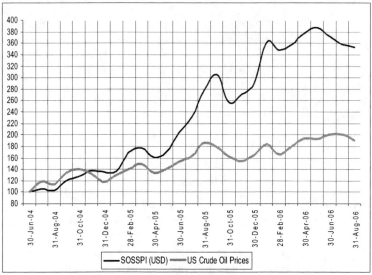

Figure #17: Appreciation of the Sustainable Oil Sands Price Index (SOSSPI on Bloomberg) vs. Crude oil Prices, June 2004 – Aug, 2006, Source: Bloomberg and SWM Ltd.

Over the next ten years, oil sands production is expected to triple or even quadruple while oil prices are expected to remain high[23] (see Figure #18 below). This will continue to benefit the stocks of Canadian oil sands producers.

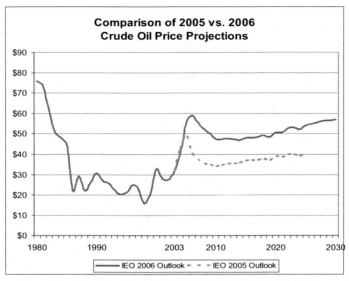

Figure #18: International Energy Outlook, 1980 to 2030 Crude Oil Price
Projections , Source: International Energy Agency, IEO 2006

As Figure #18 demonstrates, projections on future oil prices are rising. The chart indicates that the world leading authority on energy, the International Energy Agency, projects that crude oil prices will maintain above the $40 US level into the foreseeable future. This will benefit oil sands producers greatly as rising production along with higher crude oil prices will drive earnings growth upward.

Economic & Political Stability

Canada's oil sands are located in the richest province/state in North America. Alberta is Canada's richest province on a per capita income basis, leads the country in terms of growth and has the lowest unemployment rate[24]. The province also has the following benefits that are very favorable for oil sands producers.

Table #10: Alberta's Competitive Advantage

	Alberta vs. Rest of Canada & US
Provincial Sales Tax	0% - Lowest in Canada & US
Oil Sands Royalty Rate	1% until project recovers all costs, 25% thereafter
Provincial Personal & Corporate Tax	Lowest in Canada
Provincial Debt	None
Provincial Budget	Several Years of Surplus
Government Stability	Same political party for decades
Employment Opportunities	Lowest Unemployment Rate in Canada

When you compare this to other oil producing regions of the world, Alberta, Canada stands out as one of the most business friendly, geopolitically stable and profitable regions in the world to produce oil. In addition, property rights are well respected and nationalization of the oil industry is highly unlikely.

Part III: Opportunities & Risks

Capacity Limits

Perhaps the most daunting problem facing the oil sands is the lack of capacity to build these multi-billion dollar projects in an under-populated, remote northern region. The world's largest mining projects are located over 3 hours drive from the closest metropolitan city, Edmonton, Alberta. The region comprises of one of the largest municipalities in North America, a total of 68,454 square kilometers yet has less than 60,000 residents as of the 2002 census. More than half of the population is connected to the oil industry and about 45% of the population have been living in the area for over 10 years[25]. The problem comes from the $30 Billion+ in projects that are scheduled to be completed in the next 5 years and the 17,000 new jobs that will be created. Statistics indicate that for every job created at the oil sands plants, three jobs are created in the region. Currently there are 8,000+ workers who are based in camps around the oil sands projects that are not even counted in the population figures mentioned above.

The key concerns about capacity include:

> Housing for temporary construction workers
> Getting skilled workers for the projects
> Escalating living costs
> Lack of social infrastructure

Temporary housing for the thousands of construction workers is a must when you have a large influx of workers. The facilities are built by the oil sands companies and tend to be dormitory style with small private rooms and communal eating and recreational facilities (see Figure #19 below). House construction cannot meet the demand for permanent housing despite the 70% growth rate in 2005. City officials are concerned that the growth of worker camp housing will lead to increased crime and social problems in the area.

One company, Canadian Natural Resources has found a unique solution to the problem of housing during the construction of its Horizon Project. Horizon is expected to complete all phases of construction by 2012 at which time it will hit production capacity of 232,000 boe/day of synthetic crude oil. The workers necessary for the construction phase include 6,000 temporary workers and 2,400 will be required to operate and maintain the project permanently after construction is completed[26].

The company is responding to this capacity issue by building new housing facilities near the construction site and a private runway to fly workers in from other regions such as depressed mining towns in British Columbia. This has the affect of reducing housing pressure in the area while providing benefit to other regions of the country that already have existing housing and but require employment opportunities for their skilled labour.

Figure #19: Horizon Project Temporary Housing, Photo: Canadian Natural Resources Ltd.

Employment Issues

The labour shortages in Canada's oil sands region are a growing concern for oil sands producers and government officials. Alberta is one of Canada's fastest growing regions with the lowest unemployment rate in the country. A recent government report estimated that over 400,000 jobs will be created in the province over the next 10 years yet only 300,000 new workers are expected to enter the work force[27]. This will put increased pressure on existing skilled workers that are required to build the oil sands projects. Companies will face tremendous problems retaining their best workers and must plan for sharply higher employment expenses to remain competitive.

The Alberta government is attempting to address the problem with a major campaign to improve the labour pool in the province. The provincial government's labour force development strategy is designed to:

> **Improve the supply of appropriately skilled workers**
> **Develop highly skilled & educated workforce**
> **Encourage the use of technological innovation**

The government hopes to achieve their goals by providing helpful labour market information, supporting skills upgrading programs, promoting apprenticeship and industry training programs, and providing education grants for low income Albertans.

Despite these initiatives, the labour market will remain constrained as the baby boom generation begins to retire over the next 10 to 20 years. At some point the province and the labour unions will have to consider the option of allowing the immigration of skilled workers from around the world in order to satisfy the estimated labour market shortage of 100,000 workers over the next 10 years.

Environmental Issues

Environmental issues threaten to delay or permanently halt further oil sands development if not addressed. The Pembina Institute, a leading advocate of environment issues in the oil sands, published a comprehensive assessment of the current state and future environmental prospects for the industry. The paper entitled, _Oil Sands Fever, The Environmental Implications of Canada's Oil Sands Rush,_ was extremely well researched and documented dissertation on the impact of the oil sands on the environment.

The report identifies the impact of irresponsible demand in North America as one of the main concerns[28]. The abundance of Canada's oil sands is being portrayed as a source of cheap and locally available oil that will meet North American demand for transportation fuels. The report correctly points out that even rapid development of Canada's oil sands will not keep pace with expanding demand for crude oil and that the real problem is the inefficient transportation system we have grown accustomed to in North America. Fuel efficiency peaked in 1986 at 10.7 L per 100 km but 20 years later we are using an average of 11.2 L per 100 km[29]. Since 72% of a barrel of crude oil is used for transportation fuel, it is clear that improving fuel economy would have a dramatic impact on our need for oil.

The key environmental concerns outlined in the report are as follows:

> **The use of a clean burning fuel (natural gas) to extract & refine a dirty fuel (bitumen)**

> **Escalating Greenhouse Gas Emissions**

> **Escalating Use of water resources**

> **Air & Water Pollution**

> **Use of Natural Gas**

Figure #20 clearly illustrated that natural gas usage by oil sands producers is unsustainable in the long term. Based on current trends, natural gas usage for oil sands production will triple in the next 15 years and represent over 28% of our Canadian production by 2020[30]. The economic loss of consuming a clean burning fossil fuel like natural gas to produce a low quality, high carbon content fuel (bitumen) will be in the billions of dollars per annum. In addition, natural gas supply growth is slowing in North America[31], yet consumer demand for electric power generation and heating of residences and businesses continues to climb[32]. At some point we will have to resolve this issue. To remain competitive future oil sands producers will work to become independent of natural gas to produce bitumen. This has already begun with the next generation oil sands project under construction by Nexen and OPTI Canada at Long Lake which converts a low value product (petroleum coke) into a valuable resource.

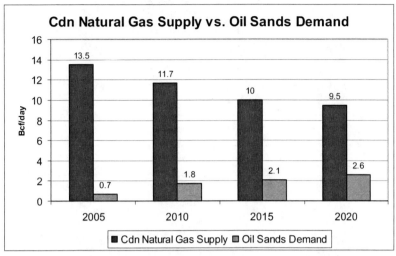

Figure #20: Canadian Natural Gas Supply vs. Oil Sands Demand, 2005 - 2020, Source: NEB, AEUB, Sustainable Wealth Management Ltd estimates.

Greenhouse Gas (GHG) Emissions

Ever since the Kyoto Protocol of 1997, greenhouse gas (GHG) emissions have been in the spotlight. Unfortunately, Canada is one of the world's largest producers of GHG and the oil sands are the single largest contributor to the problem. Despite an improvement in the emissions intensity per barrel of production of over 26% in the past decade, increased production is increasing the total GHG emitted by the oil sands. As of 2000, oil sands production represented 3% of Canada's total GHG emissions (23 Mt), a 45% increase over the level calculated in 1997 for the Kyoto Protocol[33].

Scenario and fuel type	Annual reduction in GHG intensity	2015 – annual GHG emissions (megatonnes)	2030 – annual GHG emissions (megatonnes)
Scenario 1 – natural gas	2.3%	57	83
Scenario 2 – natural gas	1%	66	118
Scenario 3 – oil sands residue (e.g., coke)	2.3%	94	138
Scenario 4 – oil sands residue (e.g., coke)	1%	97	175

Table #11: Estimates of Future GHG Emissions, Source: Pembina Institute[34]

Table #11 shows that under the worst case scenario, that the oil sands would represent over 22% of Canada's current GHG emissions by 2030. Another issue is related to the solution to natural gas usage mentioned in the previous section. Gasification of coke residue would increase GHG emissions by over 50% vs. the continued use of conventional natural gas.

An additional concern is the increasing mix of oil sands production as a % of Canada's total crude oil production. Figure #21 compares the GHG intensity of conventional oil production vs. oil sands synthetic crude oil production. For every barrel of synthetic crude oil from Canada's oil sands produced, three times as much GHG are released into the atmosphere. Currently, Canada's oil production is 50% conventional, 50% oil sands, however, the mix is expected to be 80% oil sands and 20% conventional by 2020. This is a global trend as conventional oil production is flat, while unconventional production from oil sands is increasing. As world production of oil shifts toward more unconventional sources, the emission of GHG will accelerate in the future.

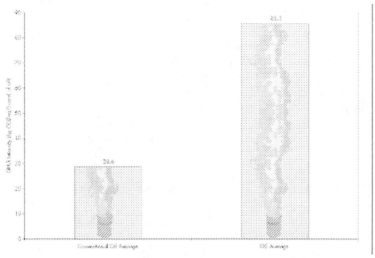

Figure #21: Average GHG Intensity Conventional Oil vs. SCO from Oil Sands, Source: Pembina Institute[35]

As a final note on this topic, the cost of complying with the Kyoto protocol by large Final Emitters (LFE) such as the oil sands projects is minor. Buying emissions credits adds less than $0.35 per barrel using a $15/tonne of CO_2 emission cost[36]. Given that oil prices continue to trade above $60 per barrel, this will have no material impact on the oil sands producers. Solutions for this issue will be focused on technological advancements. A promising proposal involves the sequestration of CO_2 emission by injecting it back into conventional oil and gas wells. This will have the added benefit of increasing production from these old conventional oil and gas fields. Additional infrastructure investment will be required but it is feasible to implement with current technology today. In order to make this approach economically attractive, the costs of complying with the Kyoto protocol would have to increase significantly to justify the investment or regulations would have to be imposed by government to force compliance.

Water Usage

Water usage by oil sands producers is tremendous and will grow in lock step with increased production, given the current extraction technology. The water used by oil sands producers comes from two sources; surface and groundwater. The biggest source is surface water. Surface water comes primarily from lakes and rivers with the majority coming from the Athabasca River. The river is over 1,538 km long, making it the longest river in Alberta and it flows into Lake Athabasca. Surface mining of oil sands requires between 2 to 5 barrels of water per barrel of oil produced. The companies are permitted to draw 2.2 billion barrels of water from the river each year and it has been estimated that only 10% of the water approved for withdrawal is returned to the river[37].

Water recycling is in widespread use in the oil sands sector and companies like Imperial Oil only require 5% fresh water for their Cold Lake operations. The biggest issue with water recycling is purifying the water so it does not damage the steam generators. Other companies use only brackish water from underground aquifers and recycle the water from tailing ponds for their operations. Despite the widespread use of water recycling, demand will continue to grow as oil sands production grows, and advanced technological alternatives to water-based extraction technology will not be available for decades to come.

Air & Water Pollution

GHG emissions are not the only environment concerns from oil sands production. Waste water from the extraction process is usually collected into massive pools called tailings ponds. The waste contains leftover bitumen, water, sand, silt and fine clay particles. The ponds cover over 50 square km in the Athabasca region and the dykes that contain them are some of the largest dams in the world. As the sand, silt and clay settle to the bottom of the ponds, the water is pumped back to the oil sands facilities to be used again in the extraction process. The major problem posed by the tailings ponds is the pollution caused by the residual bitumen and heavy elements. The pollutants have the potential to leak into the surrounding soil and surface water.

A solution to the problem is being developed by Titanium Corp which has invested over 4 years in research and development on a proprietary technology that can recover valuable heavy minerals such as titanium and zircon. According to a recent company presentation they believe that the oil sands have the potential to be the world's most valuable deposit of titanium and zircon[38]. Recovering a valuable resource and eliminating a major water contaminant is a tremendous long term benefit and I hope that other companies will follow Titanium Corporation's lead.

Another water related problem is the tendency of nearby regions to experience lower groundwater levels as multiple mines pump water from an aquifer. Over the next 15 years, water usage by all oil sands projects is expected to triple, equivalent to the water needs of a large city of 6,000,000 inhabitants.

Air pollution from Canada's oil sands producers is a growing concern. Already, Alberta is in the #1 spot in the country for air releases from industrial sources, ahead of the heavily-industrialized province of Ontario. The two major air pollutants from the oil sands are nitrogen oxide and sulphur dioxide.

Figures #22 & #23 demonstrate that oil sands production more than doubles the emissions of these key air pollutants vs. conventional oil production. Currently, the air quality of the region is similar to the metropolitan centers of Calgary and Edmonton in the south but this is unlikely to remain the case when production triples over the next 15 years.

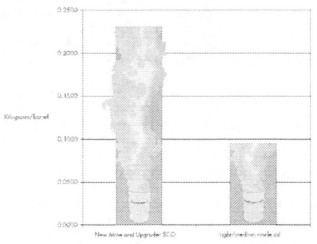

Figure #22: Nitrogen oxide emissions, conventional oil vs. oil sands
Source: The Pembina Institute[39]

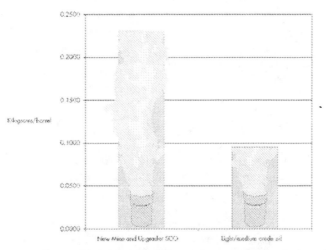

Figure #23: Sulphur Dioxide emissions, conventional oil vs. oil sands Source: The Pembina Institute[40]

Geopolitical Issues

The geopolitical environment strongly favours the development of Canada's oil sands resource. According to the Energy Information Administration, the official energy watchdog of the US government, eight of the major exports of oil to America are experiencing geopolitical instability[41].

As Table #12 demonstrates, these eight hotspots are responsible for over 35% of world oil production and represent 40% of total US oil imports. Other hotspots that would impact the global world market include Iran, Sudan, Indonesia and Libya.

In comparison, Canada is geopolitically stable and shares long standing trade relationships with the US. In addition, the energy infrastructure of the US and Canada are linked by a network of pipelines, shipping and storage facilities and refineries. Currently, Canada is the largest supplier of oil and natural gas to the United States.

Table #12: World Energy Hotspots, Source: Energy Information Administration

Country/Region	Current Oil Production	US Oil Imports	Threats
Algeria	1,900,000 bbl/d	414,000 bbl/d	Armed militants have confronted government forces
Colombia	551,000 bbl/d	110,000 bbl/d	Oil exports subject to attack by militants & protestors
Ecuador	535,000 bbl/d	316,000 bbl/d	Political instability, protests against oil exports
Iraq	2,025,000 bbl/d	516,000 bbl/d	236 attacks on Iraqi oil infrastructure, April 03 to May 05
Nigeria	2,500,000 bbl/d	1,071,000 bbl/d	Income disparity, violent crime, ethnic conflict, suspended oil exports from strikes/protests
Russia	9,300,000 bbl/d	419,000 bbl/d	Uncertain investment climate
Saudi Arabia	10,400,000 bbl/d	1,614,000	Terrorist attacks on oil workers, stability of al-Saud ruling family
Venezuela	2,900,000 bbl/d	1,579,000 bbl/d	Political animosity, potential nationalization of oil industry
Totals	30,111,000 bbl/d	6,039,000 bbl/d	
Canada	3,047,000 bbl/d	1,742,000 bbl/d	Largest source of US oil imports, ahead of Saudi Arabia and Mexico

Global Oil Demand & Supply

Growing global oil demand and a lack of stable and increasing conventional oil supply is driving the development of Canada's oil sands. Figure #24 illustrates the global energy demand projections to 2030[42]. Over the next two decades renewable energy sources such as solar, wind and geothermal will experience rapid growth, but will fail to gain any significant market share of the total world energy demand and supply. Crude oil will lose market share to coal and natural gas, however, the combined market share of the top three fossil fuels will continue to exceed 85% in 2030 and crude oil will continue to have the largest share.

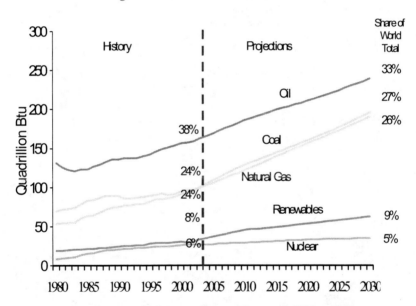

Figure #24: World Primary Energy Demand, 1980 to 2030
Source: Energy Information Administration, IEO 2006

Global energy production is highly concentrated. Figure #25 illustrates the distribution of world energy supply by country. Half of all energy production comes from just five countries of which only Canada, Russia and Saudi Arabia produce a surplus that is exported to other consuming nations. Canada is blessed with an abundance of all three of the primary energy sources, coal, natural gas and oil, and is a major exporter of all three to the US. In addition, Canada has a stable population and a mature economy that will moderate future increases in energy consumption, and allowing for further energy export growth. Saudi Arabia has a rapidly growing population with escalating local energy demand for water desalination plants and electrical demand. Concerns over the stability of the ruling al Saud family and difficulties in expanding oil production create a degree of uncertainty about Saudi Arabia's ability to increase exports in the future. Lastly, Russian energy production is dependent on continued inflows of investment capital from foreign investors. The Russian government's treatment of Yukos (Russia's largest exporter of oil that was forced into bankruptcy over tax issues) calls into question the safety of foreign investment in Russia's energy industry.

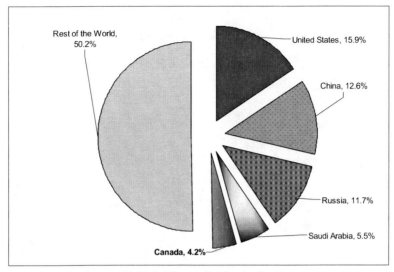

Figure #25: Global Energy Production by Country
Source: Energy Information Administration, IEO 2006

According to the International Energy Agency, oil demand in 2005 exceeded 82.5 million barrels per day. This is an 18.6% increase over 1995 oil demand of 69.5 million barrels per day. The last three years of data indicate that demand is increasing at 2.2% per annum, significantly higher than the historical average of 1.7% per year. Projecting oil demand out to 2015 using the more conservative growth rate means that oil demand will approach 102 million barrels per day, an increase equivalent to the current production of Saudi Arabia and Russia combined. Figure #26 compares the projected oil demand of the top ten users in 2015 vs. the rest of the world. The biggest increase is expected from China which will increase current demand from 7 million bbl/day to 14.5 million bbl/day.

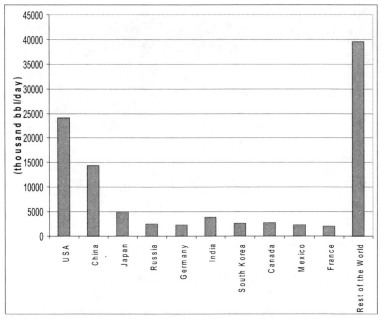

Figure #26: World Oil Demand by Country, 2015 Projection
Source: BP Statistical Review 2006, IEA, SWM Ltd. estimates

Global oil supply is just as concentrated as demand. Figure #27 illustrates the distribution of world oil supply by country. Over 60% of all oil production comes from the top ten countries of which only eight produce a surplus that is exported to consuming nations. China and the USA are net importers of crude oil from other countries and that fact is unlikely to change by 2015 given current demand trends.

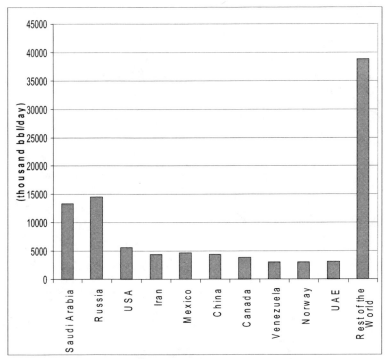

Figure #27: World Oil Supply by Country, 2015 Projection
Source: BP Statistical Review 2006, IEA, SWM Ltd. estimates

If the world continues to demand 2% more oil each year, then the majority of the world's major oil producers will struggle to keep up. Figure 28 illustrates the historical crude oil production growth of the major oil exporting countries. Only Canada and Russia appear to have the ability to match global oil demand growth and will likely gain market share over the next decade. The US is expected to continue increasing imports into the foreseeable future as their national production of oil continues to decline at about 2% per year. Current US oil imports average 15 million barrels per day but will climb to over 21 million barrels per day by 2020. Canada will be in an excellent position to increase exports to the US as oil sands production increases to 4 million barrels per day over the next 15 years.

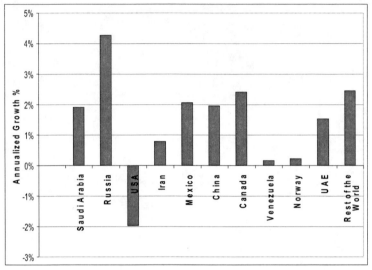

Figure #28: Annualized Oil Supply Growth by Country, 1995 to 2005
Source: BP Statistical Review 2006, IEA

New Technology

Technology will determine the ultimate value of the Canadian oil sands resource. Presently only 10 to 15% of Canada's oil sands resource of 1.7 trillion barrels is economically recoverable using current technology and given the prevailing pricing environment. Over the next twenty years new technologies will help increase this recovery factor dramatically. For every 1% improvement in oil sands recovery rate there is an additional 17 billion barrels of reserves added. To put this into perspective, America's proven recoverable reserves are estimated at 22 billion barrels. Never before in the history of the energy industry has research and development investments held the potential for such a high rate of return.

Unfortunately, investment in new technology for oil sands extraction is receiving little attention and even less money. Researchers at the University of Calgary (where Dr. Roger Butler created the SAGD process) operate on less than $10 million dollars per year and are funded primarily by government sources. The majority of oil sands producers are focusing their investment on development and engineering research for existing extraction technologies but little is being invested in more advanced approaches.

At some point in the future, the focus will have to change in order to deal with mounting operational and environmental issues mentioned in the previous chapters. New oil sands extraction technology will have a smaller surface footprint, require less energy and water resources and will have substantially lower environmental impact on the area. The following list outlines research that has the potential to achieve these goals:

➢ Expanding Solvent SAGD
➢ Clean coke gasification
➢ In Situ Refineries
➢ Nano Catalyst

According to Dr. Pedro Pereira-Almao, Co Head of the Alberta Ingenuity Centre of In Situ Energy, the future of oil sands extraction will be the development of advanced technology that will reduce or eliminate the use of natural gas and water and partially upgrade the raw bitumen to higher quality crude oil before it reaches the surface[43].

A process being developed by Petrobank Energy & Resources called the THAI (Toe to Heal Air Injection) is working toward developing the in situ refinery. Instead of using steam to heat the bitumen reservoir, THAI injects air and ignites a combustion wave that sweeps the bitumen up the pipeline. The combustion wave also partially upgrades the bitumen so that it can travel via pipeline once it reaches the surface. This process promises to eliminate the need for diluent and does not require natural gas since there is no steam injection. Figure #29 illustrates the process in the bitumen reservoir.

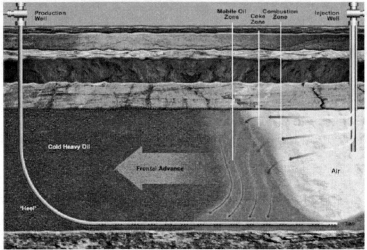

Figure #29: Diagram of the THAI in situ extraction process.
Source Petrobank Energy & Resources Ltd.[44]

For now we will have to be satisfied with the slow and steady progress of improvements in operating efficiencies and economies of scale from oil sands producers. Technological advancements in the future will unlock the vast majority of Canada's oil sands in a sustainable and environmentally benign way.

Part IV: Investing in Canada's Oil Sands Producers

Sustainable Oil Sands Sector Price Index ™

The Sustainable Oil Sands Sector Price Index ™ (SOSSPI) was created in mid 2004 as a benchmark to measure stock price appreciation of the Canadian oil sands producers. Unlike traditional stock market benchmarks such as the S&P 500 or TSX Composite the SOSSPI is not based on the market capitalization of the companies in the index. The SOSSPI index is part of the next generation of stock market indices that are based on specific attributes. Each year a complete evaluation of the oil sands producers is conducted by Sustainable Wealth Management. Companies that meet the investment criteria listed below in Table #13 are included in the index.

Table #13: SOSSPI Index Selection Criteria

Index Criteria	Minimum Value
Canadian based oil sands producer	Must be headquartered in Canada
Expected 2015 oil sands production	Must exceed 25,000 boe per day
Focus on oil sands production by 2015	Must exceed 35% of all energy production
Average daily market liquidity	Must exceed $2,000,000 CAD per day
Market Capitalization	Must exceed $500,000,000 CAD

All the companies that pass the initial screening process are evaluated according to their specific oil sands related attributes and the weightings of each company are determined according to a fixed mathematical formula each year. Table #14 illustrates the key attributes that are used to determine the index weightings.

Table #14: SOSSPI Index Attributes

Attributes	Impact on Index Weightings
Current Oil Sands Production	Current producers have higher weightings in the index
Projected 2015 oil sands production	Higher Production results in higher weightings
Focus on oil sands production by 2015	Higher focus results in higher weightings
Average daily market liquidity	Greater liquidity results in higher weightings
Market Capitalization	Greater market capitalization results in higher weightings

Traditional indices allocate the weightings of each company according to their size as measured by their market capitalization. This approach can be detrimental to index investors when a particular stock or group of stocks has a strong performance. For instance, technology stocks represented over 30% of the S&P 500 index in early 2000 and Nortel represented 35% of the TSX Composite at its peak in September 2000[45]. Currently, the energy sector represents over 30% of the TSX Composite but it is less than 10% of the S&P 500 index[46]. Another issue with traditional market capitalization based indices is that the majority of your money is not invested in the smaller, faster growing companies.

Table #15 compares the traditional S&P/TSX Capped Energy Index of Canadian energy stocks vs. the SOSSPI Index of Canadian oil sands producers.

Table #15: SOSSPI Index vs. S&P/TSX Capped Energy Index[47]

	SOSSPI Oil Sands Index	S&P/TSX Capped Energy Index
Price Appreciation Since June 30, 2004	193.1%	102%
% of index in oil sands producers	100%	67.9%
Number of Companies in the Index	17	65
% of Index in the Top Ten Holdings	73.7%	61.3%
Largest Individual Company Position in the Index	11.0%	13.6%
Smallest Individual Company Position in the Index	2.0%	0.1%

Note: All calculations are based on Aug 31, 2006 information

Considering that all the companies included in the SOSSPI index are also included in the S&P/TSX Capped Energy index, this is an incredible result. The majority of the higher stock market performance can be attributed to the incredible profits that oil sands producers have generated since crude oil prices began climbing in 2002. Another significant portion of the higher returns can be directly linked to having a larger portion of the index invested in smaller, high growth companies that had very little weighting under the TSX market capitalization method. Figure #25 charts the price appreciation of the two indices. Notice that the better results achieved by the SOSSPI index coincide with the rise in oil above $50 US per barrel.

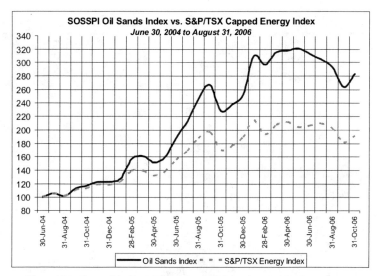

Figure #30: Chart of the SOSSPI Oil Sands Index vs. S&P/TSX Capped Energy Index. Source Bloomberg, Sustainable Wealth Management.

Key Company Profiles

The Oil Sands Sector Index includes the following 17 index constituents since the June 30, 2006 annual rebalancing.

Table #16: SOSSPI Index Constituents as of June 30, 2006

Company Name	Stock Symbol	Company Website
Canadian Natural Resources	CNQ – TSX CNQ – NYSE	www.cnrl.com
Canadian Oil Sands Trust	COS.un – TSX COSWF – PK	www.cos-trust.com
Connacher Oil & Gas	CLL –TSX CLLZF – PK	www.connacheroil.com
Encana	ECA – TSX ECA – NYSE	www.encana.com
Enerplus Resources Trust	ERF.un – T ERF – NYSE	www.enerplus.com
Husky Energy	HSE –TSX HUSKF – PK	www.huskyenergy.com
Imperial Oil	IMO – TSX IMO – AMEX	www.imperialoil.com
Nexen	NXY – T NXY – NYSE	www.nexeninc.com
OPTI Canada	OPC –TSX OPTI – BB	www.opticanada.com
Paramount Resources	POU – TSX PRMRF – PK	www.paramountres.com
Petrobank Energy	PBG – TSX PBEGF – PK	www.petrobank.com
Petro-Canada	PCA – TSX PCZ – NYSE	www.petro-canada.ca
Shell Canada	SHC – TSX SCUAF – PK	www.shell.ca
Suncor Energy	SU – TSX SU – NYSE	www.suncor.com
Synenco Energy	SYN – TSX SYEYF – PK	www.synenco.com
UTS Energy	UTS – TSX UEYCF – PK	www.uts.ca
Western Oil Sands	WTO –T WTOIF – PK	www.westernoilsands.com

Note: TSX means Toronto Stock Exchange, AMEX means American Stock Exchange, NYSE means New York Stock Exchange, BB means Nasdaq Bulletin Board listed, PK means Pink Sheets

Canadian Natural Resources

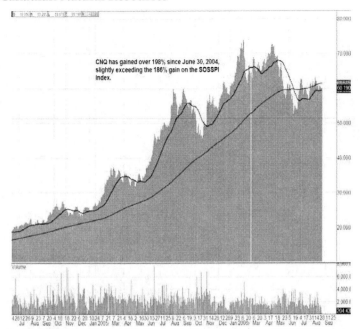

Figure #31: 2 Year Histogram of Canadian Natural Resources Stock (CNQ – TSX) Source QCharts, Sustainable Wealth Management.

Canadian Natural Resources (CNQ) is one of the most active developers of Canada's oil sands. Current production is around 56,000 boe/day from their Primrose Cyclic Steam Stimulation (CSS) in situ project. The future growth of CNQ oil sands production will come predominately from their Horizon mining and upgrade project. First production is expected to be 60,000 boe/day of synthetic crude oil (SCO) by 2008 and planned production for 2015 is expected to be 232,000 boe/day. Two additional SAGD in situ projects, Primrose East and Gregoire should come on stream in 2009 & 2012, respectively. In total, CNQ should be producing over 348,000 boe/day from all their oil sands projects by 2015, representing 10.7% of total oil sands production from the 17 companies in the SOSSPI index.

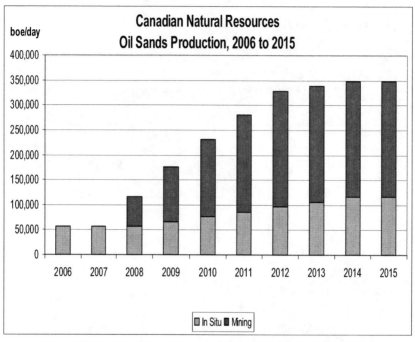

Figure #32: Canadian Natural Resources Oil Sands Production, 2006 - 2015
Source Company reports, Sustainable Wealth Management.

Investment Statistics (as of June 30, 2006)

Shares Outstanding:	537,155,000
Market Capitalization	$32.9 Billion Cdn
EPS	$4.38
P/E	13.6
Annual Revenue	$10.6 Billion Cdn
1 Year Growth in Revenue	30.5%
Annual Profit	$2.35 Billion Cdn
1 Year Growth in Profit	244%

Canadian Oil Sands Trust

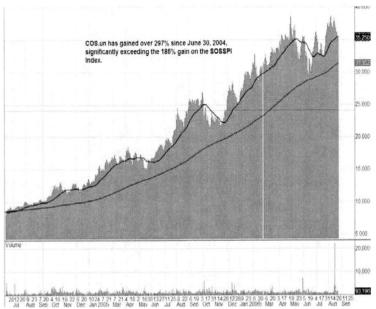

COS.un has gained over 297% since June 30, 2004, significantly exceeding the 186% gain on the **SOSSPI** Index.

Figure #33: 2 Year Histogram of Canadian Oil Sands Trust Units (COS.un – TSX) Source QCharts, Sustainable Wealth Management.

Canadian Oil Sands Trust (COS.un) is a pure play investment in the Syncrude mining project which owns 35.49% of total production. Its share of current production is 124,215 boe/day after the recent expansion phase was completed in 2006. The future growth of COS.un oil sands production will come predominately from Stage 4 expansion planned for 2010 and Stage 5 expansion in 2015. Their share of Syncrude's 2015 production should be 159,705 boe/day. This will represent about 4.9% of the total oil sands production from the 17 companies in the SOSSPI index.

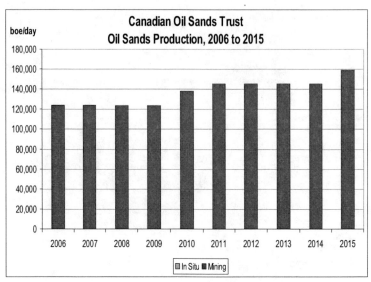

*Figure #34: Canadian Oil Sands Trust Oil Sands Production, 2006 - 2015
Source Company reports, Sustainable Wealth Management.*

Investment Statistics (as of June 30, 2006)

Trust Units Outstanding:	466,300,000
Market Capitalization	$16.8 Billion Cdn
EPS	$2.12
P/E	16.6
Annual Revenue	$2.37 Billion Cdn
1 Year Growth in Revenue	40.5%
Annual Profit	$980 Million Cdn
1 Year Growth in Profit	67.7%

Connacher Oil & Gas Ltd.

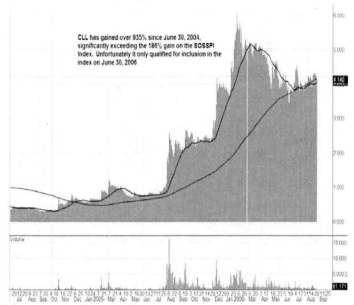

CLL has gained over 935% since June 30, 2004, significantly exceeding the 186% gain on the **SOSSPI** Index. Unfortunately it only qualified for inclusion in the index on June 30, 2006

Figure #35: 2 Year Histogram of Connacher Oil & Gas Ltd. Stock (CLL – TSX)
Source QCharts, Sustainable Wealth Management.

Connacher Oil & Gas (CLL) is one of the smaller developers of Canada's oil sands. Connacher is expecting their first production from their Great Divide SAGD project in 2008. The initial production of 5,000 boe/day is expected to increase five fold by 2012 to 25,000 boe/day. Recently, they purchased a refinery in the US that they will use to upgrade their bitumen to synthetic crude. The Great Divide project will represent 0.8% of total oil sands production from the 17 companies in the SOSSPI index in 2015.

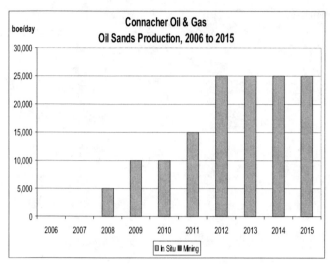

Figure #36: Connacher Oil & Gas Oil Sands Production, 2006 - 2015 Source Company reports, Sustainable Wealth Management.

Investment Statistics (as of June 30, 2006)

Shares Outstanding:	191,256,659
Market Capitalization	$822 Million Cdn
EPS	$0
P/E	n/a
Annual Revenue	$15 Million Cdn
1 Year Growth in Revenue	53.1%
Annual Profit	-$1.35 Million Cdn
1 Year Growth in Profit	-119.6%

Encana Corp

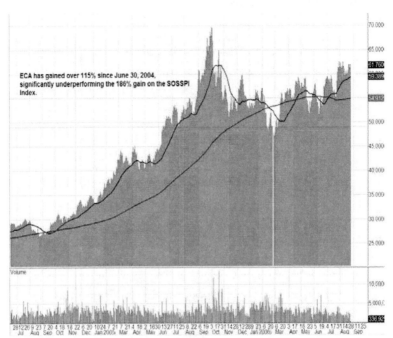

ECA has gained over 115% since June 30, 2004, significantly underperforming the 186% gain on the SOSSPI Index.

Figure #37: 2 Year Histogram of Encana Corp Stock (ECA – TSX) Source QCharts, Sustainable Wealth Management.

Encana (ECA) is one of the largest leaseholders of Canada's oil sands. Current production is around 50,000 boe/day from their Foster Creek and Christina Lake SAGD in situ projects. Encana recently entered in a joint venture with Marathon oil to use their US based refineries to process the raw bitumen they will produce from their in situ projects. The future growth of ECA oil sands production will come predominately from their expansion plans for Foster Creek (2010 completion date) and Christina Lake (2014 completion date). In addition, Encana is planning on developing their Borealis SAGD in situ process starting in 2010 and reaching full capacity in 2014. In total, ECA should be producing over 280,000 boe/day from all their oil sands projects by 2015,

representing 8.6% of the total oil sands production from
the 17 companies in the SOSSPI index.

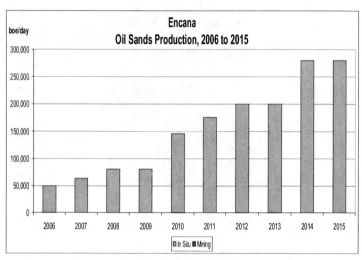

*Figure #38: Encana Oil Sands Production, 2006 - 2015 Source Company
reports, Sustainable Wealth Management.*

Investment Statistics (as of June 30, 2006)

Shares Outstanding:	815,800,000
Market Capitalization	$48.0 Billion Cdn
EPS	$8.59
P/E	7.1
Annual Revenue	$17.9 Billion Cdn
1 Year Growth in Revenue	40.8%
Annual Profit	$6.3 Billion Cdn
1 Year Growth in Profit	54.6%

Enerplus Resources Fund Trust

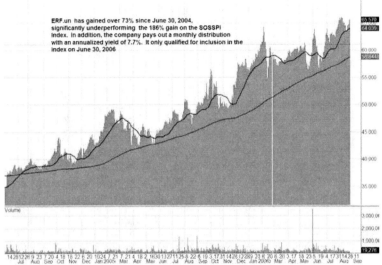

Figure #39: 2 Year Histogram of Enerplus Resources Fund Trust Stock (ERF.un – TSX) Source QCharts, SWM Ltd.

Enerplus Resources Fund Trust (ERF.un) is a minority shareholder (Total S.A.of France in the majority shareholder) in the Joslyn Mining and SAGD project. Their 15% stake in the project results in current production of 180 boe/day exclusively from the SAGD project. This is expected to climb to about 6,090 boe/day by 2012. By 2011, the mining project will begin producing with a net 1,875 boe/day and reach over 14,700 boe/day by 2015. In addition, Enerplus maintains an ownership position in a private oil sands developer named Laricina Energy Ltd. which is likely to begin producing prior to 2015. In total, ERF.un should be producing at least 20,800 boe/day from all their oil sands projects by 2015, representing 0.6% of total oil sands production from the 17 companies in the SOSSPI index.

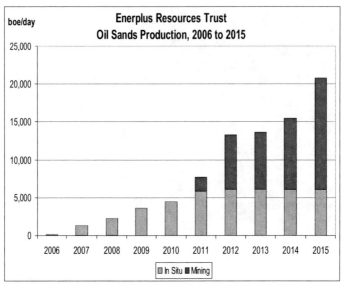

Figure #40: Enerplus Resources Fund Trust Oil Sands Production, 2006 - 2015 Source Company reports, Sustainable Wealth Management.

Investment Statistics (as of June 30, 2006)

Trust Units Outstanding:	122,582,000
Market Capitalization	$7.7 Billion Cdn
EPS	$4.60
P/E	14.2
Annual Revenue	$1.7 Billion Cdn
1 Year Growth in Revenue	43.5%
Annual Profit	$535 Million Cdn
1 Year Growth in Profit	57.8%

Husky Energy
Figure #41: 2 Year Histogram of Canadian Husky

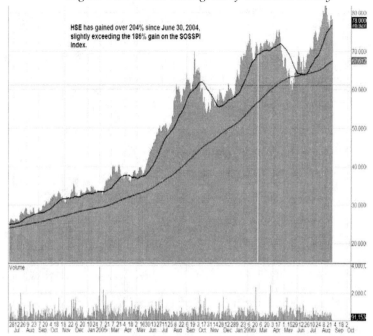

HSE has gained over 204% since June 30, 2004, slightly exceeding the 186% gain on the SOSSPI Index.

Energy Stock (HSE – TSX) Source QCharts, Sustainable Wealth Management.

Husky Energy (HSE) is an active developer of Canada's oil sands. They currently have no production but their Tucker Lake and Sunrise SAGD in situ projects are expected to start producing in 2007 and 2009 respectively. The future growth of HSE oil sands production will come predominately from their Sunrise in situ project which is expected to produce 150,000 boe/day. In total HSE should be producing over 185,000 boe/day from all their oil sands projects by 2015, representing 5.7% of total oil sands production from the 17 companies in the SOSSPI index.

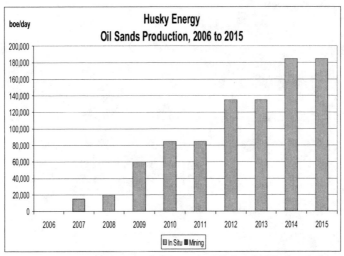

Figure #42: Husky Energy Oil Sands Production, 2006 - 2015 Source Company reports, Sustainable Wealth Management.

Investment Statistics (as of June 30, 2006)

Shares Outstanding:	424,200,000
Market Capitalization	$29.7 Billion Cdn
EPS	$6.4
P/E	12.2
Annual Revenue	$12.3 Billion Cdn
1 Year Growth in Revenue	39.8%
Annual Profit	$2.7 Billion Cdn
1 Year Growth in Profit	109.8%

Imperial Oil Ltd.

Figure #43: 2 Year Histogram of Imperial Oil Stock

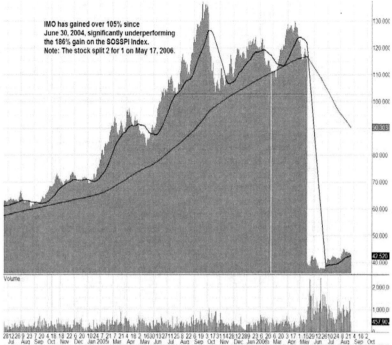

IMO has gained over 105% since June 30, 2004, significantly underperforming the 186% gain on the SOSSPI Index.
Note: The stock split 2 for 1 on May 17, 2006.

(IMO – TSX) Source QCharts, Sustainable Wealth Management.

Imperial Oil Ltd. (IMO) is one of the most active and experienced developers of Canada's oil sands. Current production is 227,500 boe/day which is coming from their Cold Lake (CSS) in situ and their 25% ownership of the Syncrude mining projects. The future growth of IMO's oil sands production will come predominately from their Kearl mining project scheduled to begin production in 2011. In total, IMO should be producing over 432,400 boe/day from all their oil sands projects by 2015, representing 13.3% of total oil sands production from the 17 companies in the SOSSPI index.

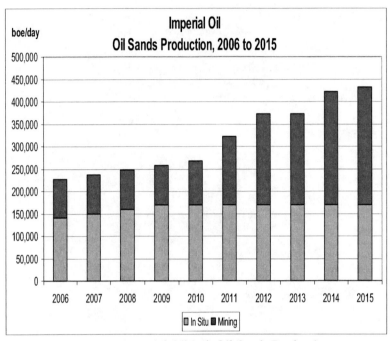

Figure #44: Imperial Oil Ltd. Oil Sands Production, 2006 - 2015 Source Company reports, Sustainable Wealth Management.

Investment Statistics (as of June 30, 2006)

Shares Outstanding:	974,076,000
Market Capitalization	$39.7 Billion Cdn
EPS	$3.09
P/E	13.8
Annual Revenue	$27.3 Billion Cdn
1 Year Growth in Revenue	15.6%
Annual Profit	$3.1 Billion Cdn
1 Year Growth in Profit	53.7%

Nexen Inc.

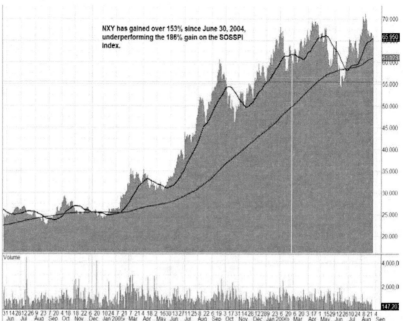

NXY has gained over 153% since June 30, 2004, underperforming the 186% gain on the SOSSPI Index.

Figure #45: 2 Year Histogram of Nexen Stock (NXY – TSX) Source QCharts, Sustainable Wealth Management.

Nexen (NXY) is a 7% owner of the Syncrude mining project and is an equal partner with OPTI Canada to develop the next generation of in situ projects. Their Long Lake SAGD in situ project includes an upgrading facility and a gasification facility that will eliminate their dependence on natural gas. The process will use a residual of bitumen/SCO called petroleum coke as the feedstock to create its own natural gas. This will result in tremendous operating cost advantages over first generation in situ projects and the company expects that operating costs per barrel will be in the $8 to $12 range long term. Production is expected to start next year and reach its peak in 2014 with 90,000 boe/day for Nexen. Future SAGD projects, Leismer and Cottonwood should come on stream in 2013 and 2015 respectively. In total, NXY should be producing over 158,300 boe/day from all their oil sands projects by 2015, representing 4.9% of total oil sands production from the 17 companies in the SOSSPI index.

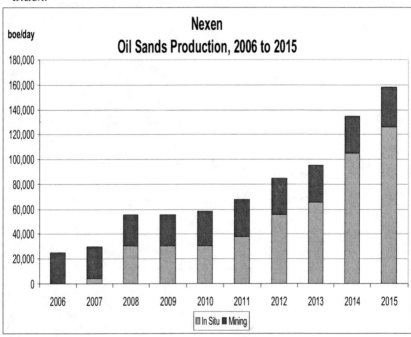

Figure #46: Nexen Inc. Oil Sands Production, 2006 - 2015 Source Company reports, Sustainable Wealth Management.

Investment Statistics (as of June 30, 2006)

Shares Outstanding:	262,142,876
Market Capitalization	$16.5 Billion Cdn
EPS	$4.76
P/E	13.7
Annual Revenue	$5.4 Billion Cdn
1 Year Growth in Revenue	31.4%
Annual Profit	$1.2 Billion Cdn
1 Year Growth in Profit	76.7%

OPTI Canada

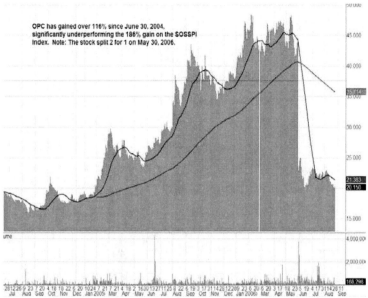

Figure #47: 2 Year Histogram of OPTI Canada Stock (OPC – TSX) Source QCharts, Sustainable Wealth Management.

OPTI Canada (OPC) is an equal partner with Nexen to develop the next generation of in situ projects. Their Long Lake SAGD in situ project includes an upgrading facility and a gasification facility that will eliminate their dependence on natural gas. The process will use a residual of bitumen/SCO called petroleum coke as the feedstock to create its own natural gas. This will result in tremendous operating cost advantages over first generation in situ projects and the company expects that operating costs per barrel will be in the $8 to $12 range long term. . Production is expected next year and will reach its peak in 2014 with 90,000 boe/day for OPTI. Future SAGD projects, Leismer and Cottonwood should come on stream in 2013 and 2015, respectively. In total,

OPC should be producing over 125,750 boe/day from all their oil sands projects by 2015, representing 3.9% of total oil sands production from the 17 companies in the SOSSPI index.

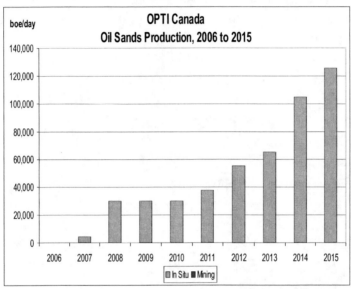

Figure #48: OPTI Canada Oil Sands Production, 2006 - 2015 Source Company reports, Sustainable Wealth Management.

Investment Statistics (as of June 30, 2006)

Shares Outstanding:	170,801,904
Market Capitalization	$3.9 Billion Cdn
EPS	-$0.01
P/E	13.6
Annual Revenue	$9.6 Million Cdn
1 Year Growth in Revenue	-46.5%
Annual Profit	-$0.5 Million Cdn
1 Year Growth in Profit	-156.8%

Paramount Resources

Figure #49: 2 Year Histogram of Paramount Resources

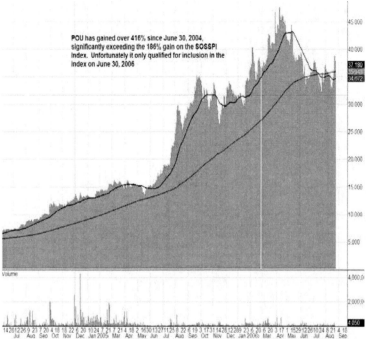

Stock (POU – TSX) Source QCharts, Sustainable Wealth Management.

Paramount Resources (POU) has a 50% ownership stake in North American Oil Sands' Kai Kos Dehseh SAGD in situ project. Production is expected to begin in 2008. Initial net production to POU is expected to be 5,000 boe/day and should quickly climb to 80,000 boe/day by 2015. This will represent 2.5% of the total oil sands production from the 17 companies in the SOSSPI index.

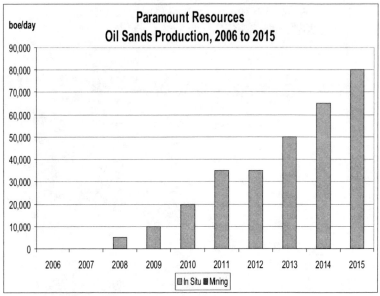

Figure #50: Paramount Resources Oil Sands Production, 2006 - 2015 Source Company reports, Sustainable Wealth Management.

Investment Statistics (as of June 30, 2006)

Shares Outstanding:	68,004,575
Market Capitalization	$2.5 Billion Cdn
EPS	$1.31
P/E	28.1
Annual Revenue	$420 Million Cdn
1 Year Growth in Revenue	-37%
Annual Profit	$88 Million Cdn
1 Year Growth in Profit	2035%

Petrobank Energy & Resources Ltd.

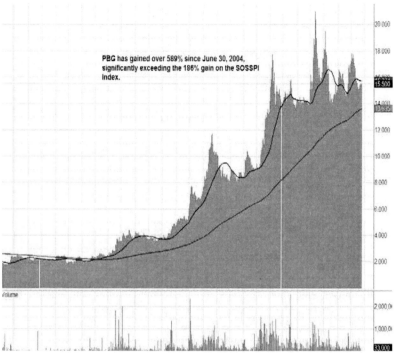

Figure #51: 2 Year Histogram of Petrobank Energy & Resources Stock (PBG – TSX) Source QCharts, Sustainable Wealth Management.

Petrobank Energy & Resources (PBG) is developing a unique in situ project using their proprietary Toe to Heal Air Injection (THAI) extraction method. First production from their Whitesands/Orion project is expected to be 10,000 boe/day of partially upgraded bitumen by 2008 and planned production for 2015 is expected to be 46,000 boe/day. If their project finds commercial success it will greatly reduce the operating cost of future oil sands projects by eliminating the need for natural gas and by upgrading the bitumen while it is still in the reservoir. PBG production will represent 1.4%

of the total oil sands production from the 17 companies in the SOSSPI index by 2015.

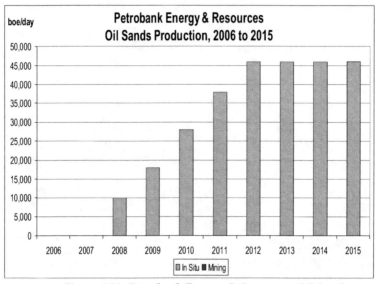

Figure #52: Petrobank Energy & Resources Oil Sands Production, 2006 - 2015 Source Company reports, Sustainable Wealth Management.

Investment Statistics (as of June 30, 2006)

Shares Outstanding:	67,257,624
Market Capitalization	$1.0 Billion Cdn
EPS	$0.37
P/E	41.9
Annual Revenue	$90.7 Million Cdn
1 Year Growth in Revenue	17%
Annual Profit	$23.7 Million Cdn
1 Year Growth in Profit	153%

Petro-Canada

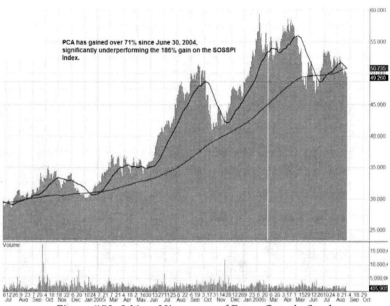

PCA has gained over 71% since June 30, 2004, significantly underperforming the 186% gain on the SOSSPI Index.

Figure #53: 2 Year Histogram of Petro-Canada Stock (PCA – TSX) Source QCharts, Sustainable Wealth Management.

Petro-Canada (PCA) is one of the most active developers of Canada's oil sands. Current production is around 68,000 boe/day from their 12% ownership of the Syncrude mining project and from their own MacKay River SAGD in situ project. The future growth of PCA oil sands production will come predominately from their 55% ownership of the Fort Hills mining and upgrade project in partnership with Teck Cominco & UTS Energy. First production is expected to be 11,000 boe/day net to PCA, growing to over 94,600 boe/day by 2015. Additional production is expected from the Meadow Creek and Lewis SAGD in situ projects with expected first production by 2009. In total, PCA should be producing over 281,600 boe/day from all their oil sands projects by

2015, representing 8.7% of total oil sands production from the 17 companies in the SOSSPI index.

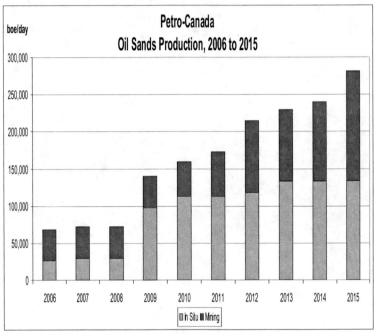

Figure #54: Petro-Canada Oil Sands Production, 2006 - 2015 Source Company reports, Sustainable Wealth Management.

Investment Statistics (as of June 30, 2006)

Shares Outstanding:	500,848,270
Market Capitalization	$26.5 Billion Cdn
EPS	$3.90
P/E	12.5
Annual Revenue	$18.8 Billion Cdn
1 Year Growth in Revenue	28.5%
Annual Profit	$2.0 Billion Cdn
1 Year Growth in Profit	52.7%

Shell Canada

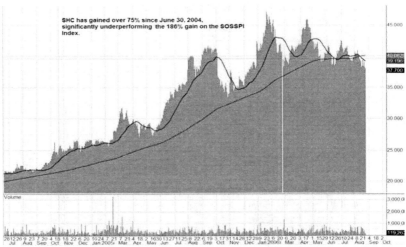

Figure #55: 2 Year Histogram of Shell Canada Stock (SHC – TSX) Source QCharts, Sustainable Wealth Management.

Shell Canada (SHC) is the majority shareholder in the Athabasca Oil Sands Project (AOSP) in partnership with Chevron and Western Oil Sands. Their 60% ownership results in net production to SHC of 99,000 boe/day. Their Peace River CSS in situ project adds another 12,000 boe/day. Both projects are being expanded aggressively over the next 10 years. Net AOSP production should be 291,000 boe/day by 2015 and Peace River production should reach 100,000 boe/day. In total, SHC should be producing over 391,000 boe/day by 2015, representing 12% of total oil sands production from the 17 companies in the SOSSPI index.

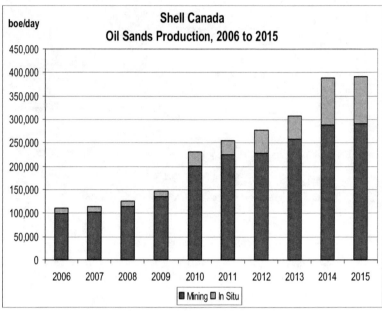

Figure #56: Shell Canada Oil Sands Production, 2006 - 2015 Source Company reports, Sustainable Wealth Management.

Investment Statistics (as of June 30, 2006)

Shares Outstanding:	825,449,564
Market Capitalization	$34.3 Billion Cdn
EPS	$2.41
P/E	15.4
Annual Revenue	$15.2 Billion Cdn
1 Year Growth in Revenue	21.3%
Annual Profit	$2.0 Billion Cdn
1 Year Growth in Profit	26.5%

Suncor Energy

Figure #57: 2 Year Histogram of Suncor Energy Stock

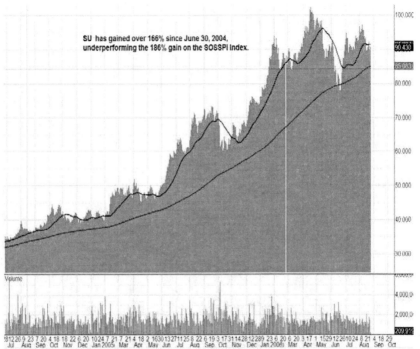

SU has gained over 166% since June 30, 2004, underperforming the 186% gain on the SOSSPI Index.

(SU – TSX) Source QCharts, Sustainable Wealth Management.

Suncor Energy (SU) is the oldest producer of Canada's oil sands. Current production is around 260,000 boe/day from their Millennium mining project and Firebag (SAGD) in situ project. The future growth of SU oil sands production will come predominately from their Voyageur mining project and the expansion of Firebag in situ project. First production is expected to be 35,000 boe/day of synthetic crude oil (SCO) by 2011 from Voyageur and planned production for 2015 is expected to be 135,000 boe/day. Firebag is expected to reach 140,000 boe/day from the current 24,000 boe/day. In total SU will continue to be the largest oil sands producer in Canada, producing over 516,000 boe/day from all their oil sands projects by 2015. This will represent 15.9% of total oil sands production from the 17 companies in the SOSSPI index. Currently, Suncor's 260,000 boe/day production represents a staggering 24.2% of Canada's oil sands production, the largest individual company position.

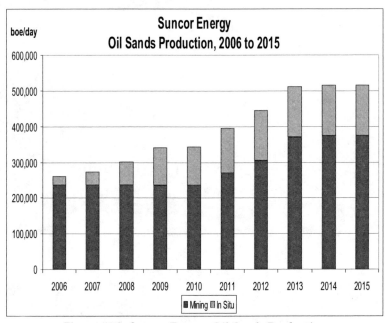

Figure #58: Suncor Energy Oil Sands Production, 2006 - 2015 Source Company reports, Sustainable Wealth Management.

Investment Statistics (as of June 30, 2006)

Shares Outstanding:	459,195,688
Market Capitalization	$41.5 Billion Cdn
EPS	$6.48
P/E	13.8
Annual Revenue	$14.7 Billion Cdn
1 Year Growth in Revenue	60.7%
Annual Profit	$2.97 Billion Cdn
1 Year Growth in Profit	261.7%

Synenco Energy

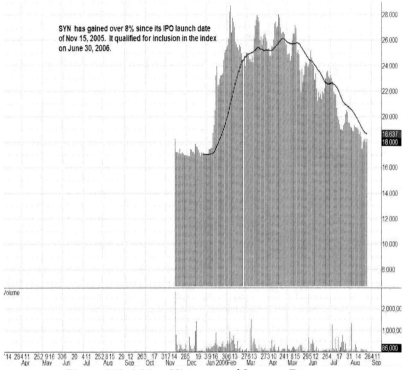

SYN has gained over 8% since its IPO launch date of Nov 15, 2005. It qualified for inclusion in the index on June 30, 2006.

Figure #59: 2 Year Histogram of Synenco Energy Stock (SYN – TSX) Source QCharts, Sustainable Wealth Management.

Synenco Energy (SYN) is a new company focused on developing Canada's oil sands. Synenco has partnered with Sinopec of China to develop the Northern Lights mining project. SYN owns 60% of the project that is expected to begin production in 2011 or 2012. Net initial production to SYN is projected to be 12,000 boe/day which should quickly increase to 60,000 boe/day by 2013. In addition, SYN also has 100% ownership of oil sands leases that they might develop on their own in the future. SYN 60,000 boe/day production represents 1.9% of total oil sands production from the 17 companies in the SOSSPI index by 2015.

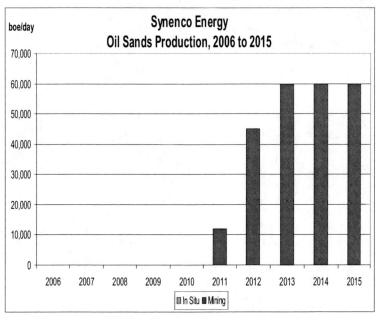

Figure #60: Synenco Energy Oil Sands Production, 2006 - 2015 Source Company reports, Sustainable Wealth Management.

Investment Statistics (as of June 30, 2006)

Shares Outstanding:	48,012,828
Market Capitalization	$1.09 Billion Cdn
EPS	-$0.21
P/E	13.6
Annual Revenue	$3.3 Million Cdn
1 Year Growth in Revenue	n/a
Annual Profit	-$5.9 Million Cdn
1 Year Growth in Profit	n/a

UTS Energy

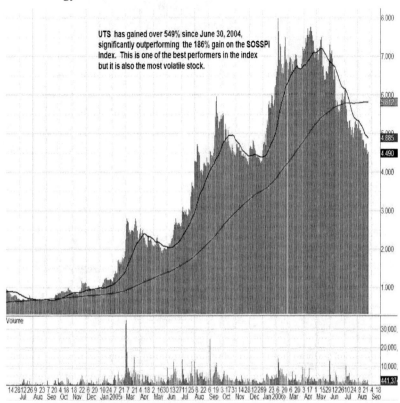

UTS has gained over 549% since June 30, 2004, significantly outperforming the 186% gain on the SOSSPI Index. This is one of the best performers in the index but it is also the most volatile stock.

Figure #61: 2 Year Histogram of UTS Energy Stock (UTS – TSX) Source QCharts, Sustainable Wealth Management.

UTS Energy (UTS) is a pure play on Canada's oil sands. UTS has a 30% ownership of the Fort Hills mining and upgrade project in partnership with Teck Cominco & Petro-Canada. First production is expected to be 6,000 boe/day net to UTS, growing to over 51,600 boe/day by 2015. This will represent 1.6% of total oil sands production from the 17 companies in the SOSSPI index. UTS is one of the best performers in the SOSSPI index but it is also the most volatile stock.

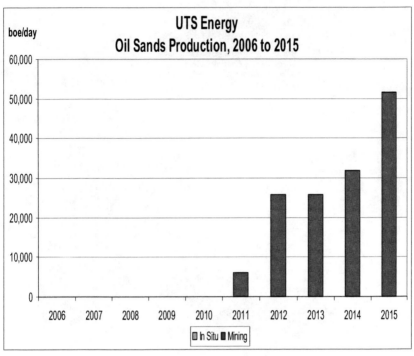

Figure #62: UTS Energy Oil Sands Production, 2006 - 2015 Source Company reports, Sustainable Wealth Management.

Investment Statistics (as of June 30, 2006)

Shares Outstanding:	424,746,073
Market Capitalization	$2.5 Billion Cdn
EPS	$0.00
P/E	n/a
Annual Revenue	$3.1 Million Cdn
1 Year Growth in Revenue	240%
Annual Profit	$1.3 Million Cdn
1 Year Growth in Profit	144%

Western Oil Sands

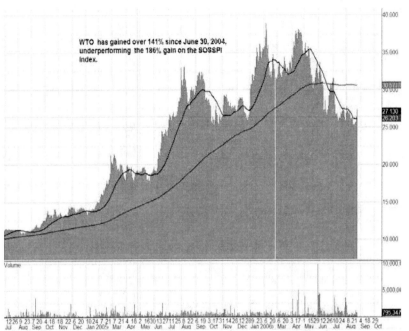

WTO has gained over 141% since June 30, 2004, underperforming the 186% gain on the SOSSPi Index.

Figure #63: 2 Year Histogram of Western Oil Sands Stock (WTO – TSX) Source QCharts, Sustainable Wealth Management.

Western Oil Sands (WTO) is the minority shareholder in the Athabasca Oil Sands Project (AOSP) in partnership with Chevron and Shell Canada. Their 20% ownership results in net production to WTO of 33,000 boe/day. AOSP is expanding aggressively over the next 10 years. Net AOSP production should be 97,000 boe/day by 2015, representing 3% of total oil sands production from the 17 companies in the SOSSPI index by 2015.

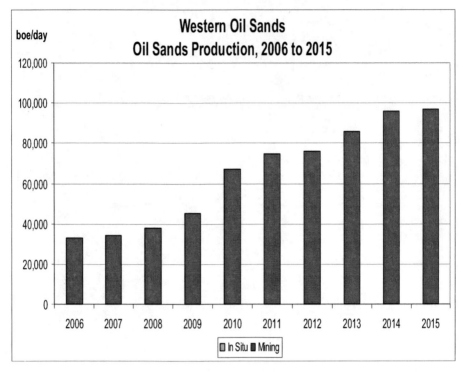

Figure #64: Western Oil Sands Production, 2006 - 2015 Source Company reports, Sustainable Wealth Management.

Investment Statistics (as of June 30, 2006)

Shares Outstanding:	161,070,149
Market Capitalization	$5.0 Billion Cdn
EPS	$0.50
P/E	54.4
Annual Revenue	$936 Million Cdn
1 Year Growth in Revenue	12.6%
Annual Profit	$78 Million Cdn
1 Year Growth in Profit	28.5%

Investing for Income & Growth

Early in 2006 a group of closed end investment funds were created to give investors direct exposure to Canada's oil sands. These funds were based on the successful income trust model and raised over $500 MM CAD from mostly retail investors at Canadian brokerage houses. The investment trusts have low distributions because most oil sands producers do not pay substantial dividends since they are reinvesting aggressively in their projects. To compensate for this and to ensure that the capital of the trusts are not depleted by distributions, the investment managers of the trust combine high yielding oil and gas trusts to the mix to boost up the distribution income. Table #17 compares the three income and growth oil sands focused closed end funds available in Canada.

Table #17: Closed end funds focused on Canada's Oil Sands

Company Name	Stock Symbol	Current Yield (Aug 31, 2006)	Assets ($ MM) (Aug 31, 2006)
Enervest Energy & Oil Sands Total Return Trust	EOS.un - TSX	6.0%	41
Oil Sands Sector Fund Trust (Markland Street/AGF)	OSF.un – TSX	5.7%	376
Sentry Select Oil Sands & Energy Mega-Projects Trust	OSM.un – TSX	5.6%	87

Source: Globeinvestorgold.com

The timing of the launch of these funds was generally poor as most of the oil sands producers have been in a flat or downtrend since their Jan and April peaks. Despite the poor timing, each fund offers varying exposure to Canada's oil sands producers and a steady stream of income that is sure to grow in the future as the oil sands producers complete major projects. The most important issue for investors is the tendency for these investments to trade below their true value (Net Asset Value per Share). As I write this in late August 2006, these investments are trading at 5% to 9% discounts to their true value. For new investors this means you are purchasing the trust unit at bargain prices, however, for existing investors this means that you are not getting full value in the market if you are required to sell at this time. Another consideration for investors is the liquidity of their investment. On a typical trading day these closed end funds trade less than 50,000 shares per day, which means that investors trying to buy or sell large amounts of these funds will experience a lack of liquidity. Currently, the biggest buyer of the units are the fund managers themselves, who are purchasing up to 10% of all the outstanding shares at today's discount prices in order to create market liquidity and to help boost the investment returns of the funds in the future.

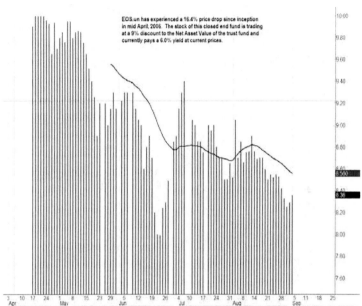

EOS.un has experienced a 16.4% price drop since inception in mid April, 2006. The stock of this closed end fund is trading at a 9% discount to the Net Asset Value of the trust fund and currently pays a 6.0% yield at current prices.

Figure #65:Enervest Energy & Oil Sands Total Return Trust Source QCharts, Sustainable Wealth Management.

Investment Statistics (as of Aug 31, 2006)

Distribution Per Unit: $0.50/unit, paid monthly at $0.0417/unit
Market Capitalization $41 Million Cdn
Net Asset Value per Unit $8.94/unit
Current Market Quote $8.14/unit
Discount to Net Asset Value   9.0%
Fund Inception Date   April 13, 2006
Total Return to Initial Investors   -16.9%
Total Return based on NAVPS   -8.9%

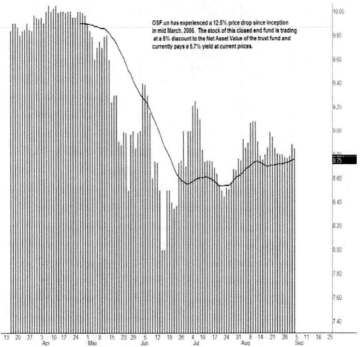

Figure #66:AGF/Markland Street Oil Sands Sector Fund Trust
Source QCharts, Sustainable Wealth Management.

Investment Statistics (as of Aug 31, 2006)

Distribution Per Unit:	$0.50/unit, paid quarterly at $0.125/unit
Market Capitalization	$376 Million Cdn
Net Asset Value per Unit	$9.39/unit
Current Market Quote	$8.89/unit
Discount to Net Asset Value	5.3%
Fund Inception Date	March 15, 2006
Total Return to Initial Investors	-9.9%
Total Return based on NAVPS	-4.9%

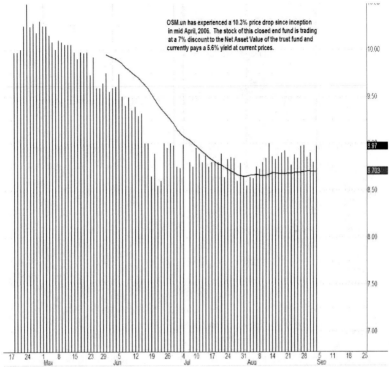

OSM.un has experienced a 10.3% price drop since inception in mid April, 2006. The stock of this closed end fund is trading at a 7% discount to the Net Asset Value of the trust fund and currently pays a 5.6% yield at current prices.

Figure #67: Sentry Select Oil Sands & Energy Mega-Projects Trust
Source QCharts, Sustainable Wealth Management.

Investment Statistics (as of Aug 31, 2006)

Distribution Per Unit:	$0.50/unit, paid monthly at $0.0417/unit
Market Capitalization	$87 Million Cdn
Net Asset Value per Unit	$9.29/unit
Current Market Quote	$8.68/unit
Discount to Net Asset Value	6.6%
Fund Inception Date	April 18, 2006
Total Return to Initial Investors	-11.5%
Total Return based on NAVPS	-5.4%

Matching the Index

The easiest and lowest cost method for matching the index is to invest in an Exchange Traded Fund (ETF). Sustainable Wealth Management Ltd. recently signed an agreement with Claymore Investments Inc. to license the SOSSPI index for exactly that purpose. The ETF is named the Claymore Oil Sands Sector ETF and will trade under the symbol CLO on the Toronto Stock Exchange starting October 26, 2006.

Compared to the closed end funds mentioned in the previous chapter, the Claymore Oil Sands Sector ETF will have the following advantages:

> ➢ Lower Management Cost
> ➢ 100% focus on Canada's Oil Sands Producers
> ➢ 100% growth oriented
> ➢ Tax efficient structure
> ➢ Market liquidity (trading support from brokerage houses & institutions)
> ➢ 100% transparency of holdings at all times

Claymore maintains a detailed website that provides investors with information on the current market price and end of day NAV of the index at the following link: http://www.claymoreinvestments.ca/ETFs/Public/etf/ETFHome.aspx.

In addition, Claymore publishes the CLO Investors Guide – Claymore Oil Sands Sector ETF which outlines the details about the ETF and the investment opportunity in the sector. The guide can be downloaded from their website at http://www.claymoreinvestments.ca/ETFs/Public/common/DisplayLiterature.aspx?ID=73941316-af28-445f-bd8d-aa1e155e22cb

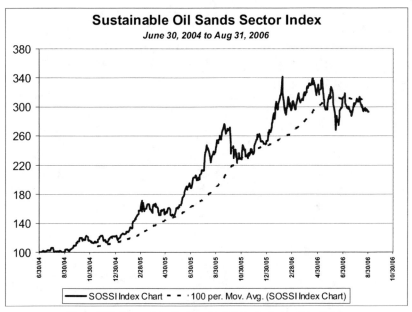

Figure #68: Chart of the Sustainable Oil Sands Sector Price Index
Source: Sustainable Wealth Management.

Beating the TSX Capped Energy Index

The S&P/TSX Capped Energy index has been one of the best performing indices over the last three years. The index gained 36.3% annually (as of the end of August 2006) according to Globeinvestor[48]. This was good enough to outperform all but 7 of its 53 resource mutual fund peers during the period. Narrowing the list to pure energy funds it outperformed all but one of its 10 peers. Many investors feel that just matching a passive index is not enough. These investors believe that specialized knowledge and a disciplined approach can outperform the benchmark index substantially. One company that is focused on outperforming the S&P/TSX Capped Energy Index is Scivest Alternative Strategies Inc. The company specializes in boosting the investment returns from any index using their award winning PLUS strategy. In early 2006, Scivest created the first fund based on the Sustainable Oil Sands Sector Index ™ which was designed to outperform the TSX Capped Energy Index benchmark.

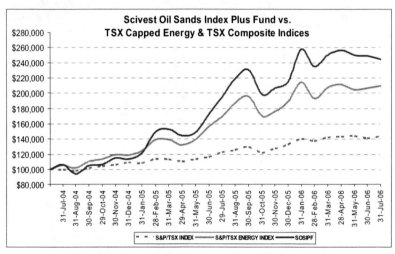

Figure #69: Chart of the TSX Composite & TSX Capped Energy Index vs. the Scivest Oil Sands Index Plus Fund(Backtested) Source: Scivest Alternative Strategies.

According to the company their PLUS strategy has the following benefits for investors:

➤ No change to existing asset allocation
➤ Capital is used more efficiently
➤ Greater diversification of portfolio risk
➤ Cost effective
➤ Reduced market timing and asset class investment decisions

PERFORMANCE COMPARISON*

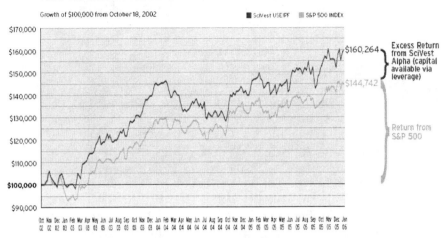

Figure #70: Performance Comparison S&P 500 Index vs. the Scivest US Equity Index Plus Fund Source: Scivest Alternative Strategies

Figure #70 shows how Scivest has consistently added value to the S&P 500 index over the last 3 years. Their fund has added an average of 3.2% per year to the S&P 500 index[49]. This is an impressive result considering that the index is the world's largest benchmark stock index by market capitalization and less than 5% of all US equity funds available in Canada were capable of outperforming the S&P index in the last three years.

Investment Statistics SOSIPF Class A units (as of Aug 4, 2006)

Net Asset Value per Unit $104.20/unit
Current Market Quote $104.20/unit
Discount to Net Asset Value 0.0% (This is an open end fund, redeemable each week at the Net Asset Value
Fund Inception Date March 10, 2006
Total Return to Initial Investors 4.2% (Aug 4, 2006 end date)

Availability: Through
investment advisors under Offering Memorandum,
investors must be accredited
Company website   www.Scivest.com

Reducing Your Risk

The Sustainable Oil Sands Sector index has
generated exceptional returns since inception, however
the risk is significantly higher than the conventional
S&P/TSX Capped energy index. Measured by standard
deviation, investors in the oil sands index are accepting
30% higher risk than the benchmark energy index. So far,
the additional risk has been offset by the 93% higher
return (see Figure #71). For those that want the higher
returns of Canada's oil sands producers but are not
willing to take the additional risk you can choose to hedge
your investment using the ETF that tracks the S&P/TSX
Capped Energy Index.

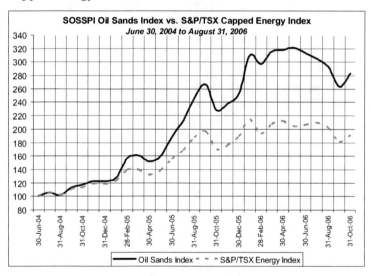

*Figure #71: Performance Comparison S&P/TSX Capped Energy
Index vs. SOSSPI Index Source: Starquote, Sustainable Wealth Management*

Table #18 demonstrates that the returns of the S&P/TSX Capped Energy Index (TTEN) are closely correlated to the SOSSPI Index. In general, the downside risk of the two indices is almost identical in both % of monthly returns being negative (31% for TTEN vs. 35% for SOSSPI) and the worst monthly returns (-13.6% for TTEN vs. -14.7% for SOSSPI). The SOSSPI index has a significantly greater average monthly return (4.3% vs 3.0% for the TTEN index) and has demonstrated higher positive returns when markets are good.

Table #18: Performance Statistics, SOSSPI vs. TTEN

Company Name	S&P/TSX Capped Energy Index (TTEN)	SOSSPI Index
Cumulative Return (Aug 31, 2006)	174.6%	102.0%
Best Monthly Return	23.4%	13.6%
Worst Monthly Return	-14.7%	-13.6%
Average Monthly Return	4.3%	3.0%
% Positive Monthly Returns	65%	69%
Standard Deviation of Returns	8.8%	6.7%

Source: Bloomberg, Sustainable Wealth Management

There is approximately a 70% overlap between the SOSSPI Index and the TTEN Energy Index. An appropriate strategy to protect yourself from an anticipated major decline in the Canadian oil sands (represented by the SOSSPI Index) is to short the iShares S&P/TSX Energy ETF (Symbol XEG on the TSX) for approximately 70% of the value of your total position in the Canadian oil sands producers. The effect of this is to reduce your net exposure to the market to just 30% or the equivalent of holding 70% cash.

The benefits to the investor are as follows:

➤ You don't have to sell your existing positions to protect from an anticipated drop, this prevents the triggering of long term capital gains and associated taxes

➤ You can quickly protect yourself with one transaction

➤ You can quickly reverse your bearish decision with one transaction

➤ If you are wrong about the anticipated drop you can still profit

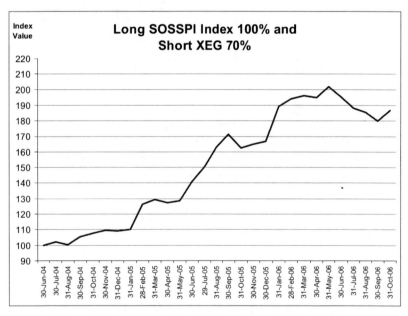

Figure #72: Hedged Portfolio, 100% invested in SOSSPI, 70% Short
in XEG Source: Bloomberg, Starquote, Sustainable Wealth Management

Figure #72 shows the returns generated by a portfolio that is 100% invested at all times in the SOSSPI index and is shorting 70% of the portfolio value using the iShares S&P/TSX Energy index ETF (symbol XEG on the Toronto Stock Exchange).

This conservative portfolio would have generated the following results to the end of August, 2006:

Cumulative Return	85.5%
Best Monthly Return	14.5%
Worst Monthly Return	-5.2%
Average Monthly Return	2.3%
% Positive Returns	67%
Standard Deviation of Returns	4.8%

Overall, this portfolio generated a 32.8% compound annual rate of return to investors yet had only 40% of the downside risk as the TSX Energy benchmark (Worst month -5.2% vs. -13.6% for the TTEN). In addition, the hedged portfolio generated a higher monthly return during its best month (14.5% vs. 13.6%) than the TTEN benchmark. In summary, the hedged oil sands portfolio generated equity market returns with bond market volatility and consistency. This strategy is ideally suited to conservative institutional investors such as pension plans and endowment funds and should be considered by risk adverse individual investors..

Conclusion

This guide has attempted to educate the reader on the tremendous investment opportunity in Canada's oil sands. We are in the beginning phases of one of the most significant increase in energy production in Canada's history. Canada is already one of the world's leading producers and exporters of the three main energy sources, coal, natural gas and oil.

The oil sands represent the largest investment opportunity in the global energy sector to date. Of the total proven reserves of 174 billion barrels, only 3% has been produced to date. In comparison, most oil producing regions are past their prime production periods and are facing declines in their conventional oil production.

Canada and the province of Alberta have implemented investor friendly tax and royalty regimes to encourage the rapid development and exploitation of the oil sands resource. Despite massive investment and the four decade long development, only 20% of all oil sands leases have been acquired so far.

Global demand for energy continues to grow at an accelerated pace as global population grows and as developing nations strive to attain the wealth and lifestyle of the industrialized nations. The reduced energy intensity of mature economies in Europe and North America will be completely offset by the rapid industrialization of China, India and Brazil. Oil will continue to dominate global energy markets and will remain the primary energy source for the transportation industry. Canada is one of the few countries that has the capacity to substantially increase its oil production to meet the growing demand.

Canada is also one of the most geopolitically stable countries in the world and has existing trading relationships and closest proximity to the largest importer of oil. The majority of the world's excess oil production and reserves are in politically and economically unstable regions of the world, namely Africa and the Middle East.

The main deterrents to future development of the oil sands are escalating costs due to capacity constraints in the skilled labour market, higher input costs (materials, natural gas, etc.) and increasing environmental damage from water and air pollution. These problems are not easily remedied but must be addressed in order to maintain the sustainability of current and future oil sands projects.

Technological advancements in oil sands extraction methods promise to reduce natural gas and water usage, reduce the environmental footprint of oil sands projects and improve the recovery rate of oil sands reserves. Investment in technology is the key to improving the economics of oil sands producers and maintaining Canada's environment.

Lastly, investors in Canada's oil sands producers must realize that they are investing in a leveraged play on the rise in crude oil prices. Volatile swings in crude oil, natural gas and even currency rates will have a major impact on investment returns. The biggest impact will come from investor sentiment towards the sector. As I write this at the end of summer 2006, you find concerns over a slowing global economy, rising oil sands development costs and reduced geopolitical tensions playing havoc with the share prices of oil sands producers. This is the opposite of the oil sands euphoria that was prevailing during the first quarter of 2006 that was punctuated by the launch of several funds in Canada investing in the oil sands sector.

Sharp downtrends in the sector will continue to plague long term investors in the future, however, I hope that this guide will remind you of the vast potential of Canada's oil sands and keep you invested during the dark times.

List of Tables

List of Figures

Glossary of Terms Used

API Gravity A specific gravity scale developed by the American Petroleum Institute (API) for measuring the relative density or viscosity of various petroleum liquids.

Area The area used to determine the bulk rock volume of the oil-, crude bitumen-, or gas-bearing reservoir, usually the area of the zero isopach or the assigned area of a pool or deposit.

Condensate A mixture mainly of pentanes and heavier hydrocarbons that may be contaminated with sulphur compounds and is recovered or is recoverable at a well from an underground reservoir. It may be gaseous in its virgin reservoir state but is liquid at the conditions under which its volume is measured or estimated (*Oil and Gas Conservation Act*, Section 1(1)(d.1)).

Cogeneration Gas-fired plant used to generate both electricity and steam.

Crude Bitumen A naturally occurring viscous mixture mainly of hydrocarbons heavier than pentane that may contain sulphur compounds and that in its naturally occurring viscous state will not flow to a well (*Oil Sands Conservation Act*, Section 1(1)(f)).

Crude Oil (Conventional) A mixture mainly of pentanes and heavier hydrocarbons that may be contaminated with sulphur compounds and is recovered or is recoverable at a well from an underground reservoir. It is liquid at the conditions under which its volume is measured or estimated and includes all other hydrocarbon mixtures so recovered or recoverable except raw gas, condensate, or crude bitumen (*Oil and Gas Conservation Act*, Section 1(1)(f.1)).

Crude Oil (Heavy) Crude oil is deemed to be heavy crude oil if it has a density of 900 kg/m3 or greater, but the EUB may classify crude oil otherwise than in accordance with this criterion in a particular case, having regard to its market utilization and purchaser's classification.

Crude Oil (Light-Medium) Crude oil is deemed to be light-medium crude oil if it has a density of less than 900 kg/m3, but the EUB may classify crude oil otherwise than in accordance with this criterion in a particular case, having regard to its market utilization and purchaser's classification.

Crude Oil (Synthetic) A mixture mainly of pentanes and heavier hydrocarbons that may contain sulphur compounds and is derived from crude bitumen. It is liquid at the conditions under which its volume is measured or estimated and includes all other hydrocarbon mixtures so derived (*Oiland Gas Conservation Act*, Section 1(1)(t.1)).

Decline Rate The annual rate of decline in well productivity.

Density The mass or amount of matter per unit volume.

Diluent Lighter viscosity petroleum products that are used to dilute crude bitumen for transportation in pipelines.

Discovery Year The year when drilling was completed of the well in which the oil or gas pool was discovered.

Economic Ratio of waste (overburden material that covers mineable ore) to **Strip Ratio** ore (in this report refers to coal or oil sands) used to define an economic limit below which it is economical to remove the overburden to recover the ore.

Established Those reserves recoverable under current technology and present and **Reserves** anticipated economic conditions specifically proved by drilling, testing, or production, plus the portion of contiguous recoverable reserves that are interpreted to exist from geological, geophysical, or similar information with reasonable certainty.

Ethane In addition to its normal scientific meaning, a mixture mainly of ethane that ordinarily may contain some methane or propane (*Oil and Ga sConservation Act*, Section 1(1)(h.1)).

Extraction The process of liberating hydrocarbons (propane, bitumen) from their source (raw gas, mined oil sands).

Feedstock In this report feedstock refers to raw material supplied to a refinery, oil sands upgrader, or petrochemical plant.

Gas Raw gas, marketable gas, or any constituent of raw gas, condensate, crude bitumen, or crude oil that is recovered in processing and is gaseous at the conditions under which its volume is measured or estimated (*Oil and Gas Conservation Act*, Section 1(1)(j.1)).

Gas (Associated) Gas in a free state in communication in a reservoir with crude oil under initial reservoir conditions.

Gas (Marketable) A mixture mainly of methane originating from raw gas or, if necessary, from the processing of the raw gas for the removal or partial removal of some constituents, and that meets specifications for use as a domestic, commercial, or industrial fuel or as an industrial raw material (*Oil and Gas Conservation Act*, Section 1(1)(m)).

Gas (Nonassociated) Gas that is not in communication in a reservoir with an accumulation of liquid hydrocarbons at initial reservoir conditions.

Gas(Raw) A mixture containing methane, other paraffinic hydrocarbons, nitrogen, carbon dioxide, hydrogen sulphide, helium, and minor impurities, or some of these components, that is recovered or is recoverable at a well from an underground reservoir and is gaseous at the conditions under which its volume is measured or estimated (*Oil and Gas Conservation Act*, Section 1(1)(s.1)).

Gas (Solution) Gas that is dissolved in crude oil under reservoir conditions and evolves as a result of pressure and temperature changes.

Gas-Oil Ratio The volume of gas (in cubic metres, measured under standard **(Initial Solution)** conditions) contained in one stock-tank cubic metre of oil under initial reservoir conditions.

Initial Established Reserves Established reserves prior to the deduction of any production.

Initial Volume in Place The volume of crude oil, crude bitumen, raw natural gas, or coal calculated or interpreted to exist in a reservoir before any volume has been produced.

Mean Formation Depth The approximate average depth below kelly bushing of the midpoint of an oil or gas productive zone for the wells in a pool.

Methane In addition to its normal scientific meaning, a mixture mainly of methane that ordinarily may contain some ethane, nitrogen, helium, or carbon dioxide (*Oil and Gas Conservation Act*, Section 1(1)(m.1)).

Natural Gas Liquid Ethane, propane, butanes, pentanes plus, or a combination of these obtained from the processing of raw gas or condensate.

Netback Crude oil netbacks are calculated from the price of WTI at Chicago less transportation and other charges to supply crude oil from the wellhead to the Chicago market. Alberta netback prices are adjusted for the U.S./Canadian dollar exchange rate as well as crude quality differences.

Off-gas Natural gas that is produced from bitumen production in the oil sands. This gas is typically rich in natural gas liquids and olefins.

Oil Condensate, crude oil, or a constituent of raw gas, condensate, or crude oil that is recovered in processing and is liquid at the conditions under which its volume is measured or estimated (*Oil and Gas Conservation Act*, Section 1(1)(n.1)).

Oil Sands (i) sands and other rock materials containing crude bitumen, (ii) the crude bitumen contained in those sands and other rock materials, and (iii) any other mineral substances other than natural gas in association with that crude bitumen or those sands and other rock materials referred to in subclauses (i) and (ii) (*Oil Sands Conservation Act*, Section l(l)(o)).

Oil Sands Deposit A natural reservoir containing or appearing to contain an accumulation of oil sands separated or appearing to be separated from any other such accumulation (*Oil and Gas Conservation Act*, Section 1(1)(o.1)).

Overburden In this report overburden is a mining term related to the thickness of material above a mineable occurrence of coal or bitumen.

Pay Thickness (Average) The bulk rock volume of a reservoir of oil, oil sands, or gas divided by its area.

Pentanes Plus A mixture mainly of pentanes and heavier hydrocarbons that ordinarily may contain some butanes and is obtained from the processing of raw gas, condensate, or crude oil (*Oil and Gas Conservation Act*, Section 1(1)(p)).

Pool A natural underground reservoir containing or appearing to contain an accumulation of oil or gas or both separated or appearing to be separated from any other such accumulation (*Oil and Gas Conservation Act*, Section 1(1)(q)).

Porosity The effective pore space of the rock volume determined from core analysis and well log data measured as a fraction of rock volume.

Propane In addition to its normal scientific meaning, a mixture mainly of propane that ordinarily may contain some ethane or butanes (*Oil and Gas Conservation Act*, Section 1(1)(s)).

Recovery(Enhanced) The increased recovery from a pool achieved by artificial means or by the application of energy extrinsic to the pool. The artificial means or application includes pressuring, cycling, pressure maintenance, or injection to the pool of a substance or form of energy but does not include the injection in a well of a substance or form of energy for the sole purpose of (i) aiding in the lifting of fluids in the well, or (ii) stimulation of the reservoir at or near the well by mechanical, chemical, thermal, or explosive means (*Oil and Gas Conservation Act*, Section 1(1)(h)).

Recovery (Primary) Recovery of oil by natural depletion processes only measured as a volume thus recovered or as a fraction of the in-place oil.

Refined Petroleum Products End products in the refining process.

Refinery Light oil products produced at a refinery; includes gasoline and **Remaining Established Reserves** Initial established reserves less cumulative production.

Sales Gas A volume of gas transacted in a time period. This gas may be augmented with gas from storage.

Solvent A suitable mixture of hydrocarbons ranging from methane to pentanes plus but consisting largely of methane, ethane, propane, and butanes for use in enhanced-recovery operations.

Successful Wells Drilled Wells drilled for gas or oil that are cased and not abandoned at the time of drilling. Less than 5 per cent of wells drilled in 2003 were abandoned at the time of drilling.

Synthetic Crude Oil A mixture of hydrocarbons, similar to crude oil, derived by upgrading bitumen from oil sands.

Ultimate Potential An estimate of the initial established reserves that will have been developed in an area by the time all exploratory and development activity has ceased, having regard for the geological prospects of that area and anticipated technology and economic conditions. Ultimate potential includes cumulative production, remaining established reserves, and future additions through extensions and revisions to existing pools and the discovery of new pools. Ultimate potential can be expressed by the following simple equation: Ultimate potential = initial established reserves + additions to existing pools + future discoveries.

Upgrading The process that converts bitumen and heavy crude oil into a product with a density and viscosity similar to light crude oil.

Zone Any stratum or sequence of strata that is designated by the EUB as a zone (*Oil and Gas Conservation Act*, Section 1(1)(z)).

Symbols
International System of Units (SI)
°C degree Celsius
d day
EJ exajoule
ha hectare
J joule
kg kilogram
kPa kilopascal
M mega
m metre
MJ megajoule
mol mole
T tera
t tonne
TJ terajoule
Imperial
bbl barrel
Btu British thermal unit
cf cubic foot
d day
°F degree Fahrenheit
psia pounds per square inch absolute
psig pounds per square inch gauge

Metric and Imperial Equivalent Units(a)

Metric Imperial
1 m3 of gas(b) = 35.49373 cubic feet of gas
(101.325 kPa and 15°C) (14.65 psia and 60°F)
1 m3 of oil or pentanes plus = 6.2929 Canadian barrels of oil or pentanes
(equilibrium pressure and 15°C) plus (equilibrium pressure and 60°F)
1 m3 of water = 6.2901 Canadian barrels of water
(equilibrium pressure and 15°C) (equilibrium pressure and 60°F)
1 tonne = 0.9842064 (U.K.) long tons (2240 pounds)
1 tonne = 1.102311 short tons (2000 pounds)

1 kilojoule = 0.9482133 British thermal units (Btu
as defined in the federal *Gas Inspection Act* (60-61°F)
a Reserves data in this report are presented in the International
System of Units (SI)..
b Volumes of gas are given as at a standard pressure and
temperature of 101.325 kPa and 15°C respectively.

Term Value Scientific notation

kilo thousand 10^3
mega million 10^6
giga billion 10^9

Notes & References

[1] Bloomberg Professional Services, NG1 <Commodity> GPO M <GO> Chart.

[2] AAPG Memoirs, Oil & Gas Journal, Raymond James Research estimates & analysis

[3] Energy Information Administration, *International Energy Outlook 2006*, Figure #26, pg 26

[4] International Energy Agency, *Oil Market Report*, September 12, 2006

[5] Alberta Oil Sands Consultations, website: http://www.oilsandsconsultations.gov.ab.ca/docs/Fact%20Sheet%20Oi l%20Sands%20History.pdf#search=%22oil%20sands%20history%22

[6] Alberta Energy & Utilities Board, *Alberta's Energy Reserves 2005 and Supply/Demand Outlook 2006-2015*, Statistical Series ST98-2006, pg. 11

[7] Alberta Energy & Utilities Board, *Alberta's Energy Reserves 2005 and Supply/Demand Outlook 2006-2015*, Statistical Series ST98-2006, pg. 10

[8] Wikipedia, API gravity, www.en.wikipedia.org/wiki/API_gravity

[9] Canadian Energy Research Institute, *Oil Sands Supply Outlook, CERI Media Briefing*, March 3, 2004, pg 4

[10] The Pembina Institute, *Oil Sands Fever, The Environmental Implications of Canada's Oil Sands Rush*, November 2005, Dan Woynillowicz, Section 2.1 Making Oil from Tar, pg 21.

[11] Oil Sands Consultations, Government of Alberta, http://www.oilsandsconsultations.gov.ab.ca/docs/Fact%20Sheet%20on %20Oil%20Sands.pdf , pg 2

[12] Oil Sands Consultations, Government of Alberta, http://www.oilsandsconsultations.gov.ab.ca/docs/Fact%20Sheet%20on%20Oil%20Sands.pdf , pg 1

[13] Long Lake Oil Sands Project, OPTI Canada & Nexen, http://www.longlake.ca/project/technology.asp

[14] ExxonMobil 2005 Annual Report, Pages 8 & 9 discusses the growth global energy needs of 50% from today's levels by 2030.

[15] Matthew R. Simmons, *Energy in the 21st Century: A Rough Ride Ahead,* February 21, 2006, Greater Kansas City Chamber of Commerce, Slides 19 to 22.

[16] John Mawdsley, P. Geol., Raymond James, *The Oil Sands of Canada: The World Wakes Up: First to Peak Oil, Second to the Oil Sands of Canada,* July 28, 2005, Pages 31 to 48

[17] The Pembina Institute, *Oil Sands Fever, The Environmental Implications of Canada's Oil Sands Rush,* November 2005, Dan Woynillowicz, Section 2.2 Fuel for the Oil Sands, pg 24 & 25.

[18] Sustainable Wealth Management Ltd., Bloomberg Professional Services. Light, Sweet Crude Oil prices were compared to bitumen oil prices over the last ten years. Bitumen traded between 50% and 90% of the value of the composite benchmark for Light, Sweet Crude and averaged 68% during the period.

[19] John Mawdsley, P. Geol., Raymond James, *The Oil Sands of Canada: The World Wakes Up: First to Peak Oil, Second to the Oil Sands of Canada,* July 28, 2005, Page 49. Mining and upgrading projects have projected rate of return of 17.8% with $42 US oil and $7.50 US per mmbtu natural gas. Smaller in situ projects have a 23% rate of return. At $60 oil, returns for mining jump to 25%, in situ 32%.

[20] ExxonMobil PERSPECTIVES, *Meeting the Energy Challenge*, December 2000, Page 2. This publication for shareholders stated that the decline rates for oil production across most of the world was 6 to 8% per year. They provided a chart that demonstrated 2 to 3% global growth of demand coupled with 4% production decline rates on existing production would require 70 MM boe/day in new production by 2010 and up to $1 Trillion in investment.

[21] Based on calculations and extrapolations made by Sustainable Wealth Management Ltd of planned projects and expansions.

[22] Alberta Energy & Utilities Board, *Alberta's Energy Reserves 2005 and Supply/Demand Outlook 2006-2015*, Statistical Series ST98-2006, pg. 38

[23] Energy Information Administration, *International Energy Outlook 2006*, Chapter #1: World Energy and Economic Outlook, Figure #11: Comparison of IEO2005 and IEO 2006, World Oil Price Projections, 1980-2030, Page 9

[24] Statistics Canada Reports, Labour Force Survey, Gross Domestic Product Report and Median Total Income by province and territory. In 2004 the median family income in Alberta was $66,400 vs. $62,500 for Ontario and $55,900 in BC. Yukon and Northwest Territories had higher incomes ($67,800 and $79,800 respectively) but are sparsely populated territories, not provinces.

[25] The Regional Municipality of Wood Buffalo, *Regional Profile 2003*, Page 2, 23, 25

[26] Canadian Natural Resources, *Horizon Oil Sands Project Brochure – November, 2006*, Page 7.

[27] Government of Alberta, *Proposed Strategy Addresses Skill and Labour Shortages*, January 31, 2006, http://www.gov.ab.ca/home/index.cfm?Page=1320

[28] The Pembina Institute, *Oil Sands Fever, The Environmental Implications of Canada's Oil Sands Rush*, November 2005, Dan Woynillowicz, pg 17 & 18.

Figure #7 demonstrates that 72% of all crude oil is used for transportation fuels. Figure #8 compares the European private-vehicle fuel use vs. the American fuel use and identifies the differential as irresponsible demand.

[29] The Pembina Institute, *Oil Sands Fever, The Environmental Implications of Canada's Oil Sands Rush,* November 2005, Dan Woynillowicz, Section 1.6 The Impacts of Irresponsible Demand, pg 17 & 18.

[30] National Energy Board, *Canada's Oil Sands, Opportunities and Challenges to 2015: An Update,* An Energy Market Assessment June 2006, pg. 16-17.

[31] Alberta Energy & Utilities Board, *Alberta's Energy Reserves 2005 and Supply/Demand Outlook 2006-2015,* Statistical Series ST98-2006, pg. 115.

[32] Alberta Energy & Utilities Board, *Alberta's Energy Reserves 2005 and Supply/Demand Outlook 2006-2015,* Statistical Series ST98-2006, pg. 121, Figure 5.31 Alberta marketable gas demand by sector.

[33] The Pembina Institute, *Oil Sands Fever, The Environmental Implications of Canada's Oil Sands Rush,* November 2005, Dan Woynillowicz, Section 3.1 Escalating Greenhouse Gas Emissions, pg 28, 29 & 30.

[34] The Pembina Institute, *Oil Sands Fever, The Environmental Implications of Canada's Oil Sands Rush,* November 2005, Dan Woynillowicz, Section 3.1 Escalating Greenhouse Gas Emissions, pg 29. Exact copy of Table #3: Scenarios for GHG emissions from oil sands in 2015 and 2030.

[35] The Pembina Institute, *Oil Sands Fever, The Environmental Implications of Canada's Oil Sands Rush,* November 2005, Dan Woynillowicz, Section 3.1 Escalating Greenhouse Gas Emissions, pg 31. Exact copy of Figure #15: Avg GHG intensity for conventional oil production versus oil sands synthetic crude oil.

[36] John Mawdsley, P. Geol., Raymond James, *The Oil Sands of Canada: The World Wakes Up: First to Peak Oil, Second to the Oil Sands of Canada,* July 28,

2005, Figure #55: Minimal Costs Associated with Kyoto Compliance, Page 55.

[37] The Pembina Institute, *Oil Sands Fever, The Environmental Implications of Canada's Oil Sands Rush,* November 2005, Dan Woynillowicz, Section 4.2.1 Troubled Waters: The Athabasca River, pg 38.

[38] Titanium Corporation, *Leading the recovery of Titanium and Zircon from Canada's oil sands,* Strategic Research Institute, Oct 5, 2006 Presentation, Houston, Texas, Slide #37 Summary.
http://www.titaniumcorporation.com/s/Home.asp

[39] The Pembina Institute, *Oil Sands Fever, The Environmental Implications of Canada's Oil Sands Rush,* November 2005, Dan Woynillowicz, Section 4.4 Environmental Impacts: Polluted Air, pg 55. Exact copy of Figure #24: Nitrogen oxide intensity of producing synthetic crude oil from oil sands versus conventional oil in Alberta.

[40] The Pembina Institute, *Oil Sands Fever, The Environmental Implications of Canada's Oil Sands Rush,* November 2005, Dan Woynillowicz, Section 4.4 Environmental Impacts: Polluted Air, pg 55. Exact copy of Figure #25: Sulphur dioxide intensity of producing synthetic crude oil from oil sands versus conventional oil in Alberta.

[41] Energy Information Administration, Official Energy Statistics for the U.S. Government,
http://www.eia.doe.gov/cabs/World_Energy_Hotspots/Overview.html , September, 2005.

[42] Energy Information Administration, *International Energy Outlook 2006,* Chapter #1: World Energy and Economic Outlook, Figure #10: World Marketed Energy Use by Fuel Type, 1980-2030, Page 8.

[43] Dr. Pedro Pereira-Almao, Co-Director, Alberta Ingenuity Centre for In Situ Energy, http://www.aicise.ca/index.html .

[44] Petrobank Energy & Resources Ltd., www.petrobank.com, copy of company slide, THAI Process.

---

[45] Toronto Stock Exchange, Bloomberg Professional Services.

[46] Bloomberg Professional Services.

[47] Bloomberg Professional Services, IXE <Index> DES and Sustainable Wealth Management Oil Sands Sector Index ™, www.oilsandsindex.com.

[48] Globeinvestor Gold, www.globeinvestorgold.com.

[49] Scivest Alternative Strategies, www.scivest.com.

ISBN 142510952-7